# WEALTH WARRIOR

---

## 8 STEPS FOR COMMUNITIES OF COLOR TO CONQUER THE STOCK MARKET

---

## LINDA GARCÍA

LEGACY
LIT

NEW YORK  BOSTON

Legacy Lit
Hachette Book Group
1290 Avenue of the Americas
New York, NY 10104
LegacyLitBooks.com
@LegacyLitBooks

Originally published in hardcover and ebook by Legacy Lit in April 2023.

First Trade Paperback Edition: April 2024

Legacy Lit is an imprint of Grand Central Publishing. The Legacy Lit name and logo are registered trademarks of Hachette Book Group, Inc.

The publisher is not responsible for websites (or their content) that are not owned by the publisher.

The Hachette Speakers Bureau provides a wide range of authors for speaking events. To find out more, go to hachettespeakersbureau.com or email HachetteSpeakers@hbgusa.com.

Legacy Lit books may be purchased in bulk for business, educational, or promotional use. For information, please contact your local bookseller or the Hachette Book Group Special Markets Department at special.markets@hbgusa.com.

Library of Congress Control Number: 2022949164

ISBNs: 978-0-3068-2848-5 (hardcover); 978-0-3068-2849-2 (trade paperback); 978-8-3068-2850-8 (ebook)

Printed in the United States of America

CW

10 9 8 7 6 5 4 3 2 1

To Elizabeth Ruiz, Benicio Ayala, Emillia Lemus, Jordan Lemus, Alexa Ramirez, Eliana Ayala, Camila García, Aide Alvarez, Genesis Ruiz, Karina Muñoz, Aliana Escalante, Alexander Cristiano, Oliver Emiliano, Dakota Darton, Stazie Darton, Mar de Luz, Camila Huijsmans, Eduardo Maytorena, and Augustina Maytorena

Wealth Warrior *is for the children.*

A Wealth Warrior is a badass who conquers emotional and financial battles to create returns that will last a lifetime.

A Wealth Warrior knows that money is a seed that must be planted to create generational and community wealth.

A Wealth Warrior embodies the understanding that this is sacred work.

We are Wealth Warriors.

# CONTENTS

# INTRODUCTION

The conversation surrounding money is the darkest underbelly of America and the system that runs it. Over the years, wealth-generating investments have been inaccessible by design for communities of color. We yearn to break the money barrier to get to the side of wealth, but we have no idea where to begin because no one we know has ever exemplified what that could look like for us. Inevitably, as we grow older, we can't help but think, *Is that even possible for someone like me?* Our families have sacrificed everything to give us a shot at a better life. Yet those endless hours of work for every single cent that hit their pocketbooks has pushed them to put the fear of God in us when it comes to protecting our family's hard-earned cash. So we learn to scrape and save and use our money to cover our basic needs and be grateful we can do just that. The goal isn't to build wealth; it's to survive. We go about life needing money, wanting money, hating money, dreading money, developing an unhealthy relationship with what should be a tool in our arsenal rather than our commander in chief. And so, instead of building wealth, we start building fear, which in turn stops us from paying ourselves first, investing our money, and allowing it to grow.

When I embarked on my own personal wealth-building journey, I had no idea that money could work for me. I focused on getting good-paying jobs to emulate what I believed would lead to financial stability, yet as soon as money hit my pocket I spent it on clothes, on shoes, on experiences, even if that meant living paycheck to paycheck and scrambling to make rent and survive. It took me years to finally stop and take a long, hard look at myself and realize that this behavior was being pushed forward by something living much deeper within me.

I dug into the trenches of my emotions and began to understand that when it came to money, I was acting like a victim. I was at the mercy of whatever money needed from me. It was overpowering me, and I was submissive to it. That shook me. I've survived a long list of hardships throughout the years, but I have always refused to be called a victim or a survivor. I like to think of myself as a warrior, but it was clear that I had yet to fully embody my warrior status when it came to my wealth. My limiting beliefs on money made it painful to accept that I desired to build wealth, yet something in me yearned for more.

As I vehemently tallied the feelings connected to my finances to begin healing my entrenched money wounds, I became obsessed with figuring out how to generate more cash. I scoured the internet for content and devoured books on financial literacy. Even though I only understood a fraction of the complex theories on those pages, I was parched for knowledge. I refused to spend the rest of my life working to make someone else rich, so I kept going, until I discovered the stock market—one of the most powerful tools we have at our disposal to break free from our scarcity mindset and generate real, long-term wealth.

The stock market will not discriminate against you because

of your last name or the color of your skin or your religion or your identity. You don't need a high credit score or a lot of money to get started. This is sacred work that goes beyond simple figures. So, instead of running for the hills at the mention of the stock market, I want you to plant yourself firmly in a warrior stance and prepare to push boundaries. The system, the limiting false beliefs, our money wounds, and rocky emotions are all encroaching on us, stifling us, attempting to stop us from making the money moves that will generate the wealth we deserve. But we are badass warriors who must stand our ground and start fighting back. Welcome to your wealth-generating boot camp.

*Wealth Warrior* will provide you with the down-and-dirty stock market basics to get you started on your very own wealth-building journey. It's filled with essential explanations exploring staple terms and key financial moves, such as how to open a brokerage account, understand and choose the right stocks for you, and create a long-term investment plan, all while also revealing and healing your intergenerational money wounds. The goal of this logical and emotional step-by-step guide is for you to become familiar with the foundational elements that make up the stock market so that you can enter this space with confidence and ease and finally tap into the enormous opportunity within your reach.

As someone who embarked on my own wealth-building journey ten years ago and had to crawl through the muck of my money wounds and peel back the layers of this new world on my own, I'm now ready to share my successes, failures, and life-changing lessons so that your path to wealth may be just a little bit smoother than my own. My intention is to serve as your resource, your best friend, your tía, your sister in arms, so that you too can learn to make research-led decisions rather than allowing your emotions to take the helm. I will be your guide, but the stock market will be your ultimate teacher, your mirror. It will clearly reflect the thoughts, fears, and doubts, that are holding you back from generating more wealth. At times you may feel overwhelmed, fearful, frustrated, anxious, tearful... other times you may be overcome by a wave of exhilaration and excitement like no other. Learning how to navigate your emotions will be an essential part of becoming an astute investor.

Take it slow. Be compassionate with yourself. Don't be afraid to go back and reread different steps or look up concepts in the glossary until this new language begins to sink in and feel comfortable.

The act of incorporating these new terms, ideas, and mindsets into your everyday vocabulary and pursuing the understanding of how money works will eventually rewire your brain and change the way you perceive it. You will start viewing money from a fresh perspective that will likely inspire you to take the leap into wealth-generating investments you never thought were accessible to you in the past. What will pull you through these battlefields is the clarity, power, and confidence you gain through knowing how to move out of your own way and not let fear, negative self-talk, or other people's beliefs block you from owning your wealth-building path. As you charge forward and grasp the energy and language of money, a life of abundance will unfold before you.

Now, when someone asks me, "Why do you want so much?" rather than allowing that question to make me falter and doubt my decisions, I answer with resolve: "Because I can hire women of color and help remedy the equal pay gap, I can give to the foundations and charities I believe in, and I can redistribute my wealth as I see fit and be the example of what it means to bring big money home to my people." And that's what I want for all of us. I'm sick of being alone in the stock market. Money needs to be in the hands of people like us. That's the mission.

Join me in courageously demonstrating what is possible and within our reach when we readjust our perception of money, learn this new language of wealth, and start making sharp money moves in the stock market. I want us to communicate, connect, form alliances, and strategize, so that we can face these simultaneous battles together, break through the scarcity mindset barriers, and come out triumphant on the other side. I want to see you win, I want to see you not stress over money, and I want to see you provide much more than the essentials to your children and family. I'm not here to make you rich; I'm here to help you build long-term wealth. The amount you amass will be solely up to you and your circumstances. My intention is to help you create the necessary foundation to start your own construction and eventually turn it into a three-story building or a high-rise. Generational wealth starts with you! Are you with me?

# WEALTH
# WARRIOR

# WAKE UP TO YOUR MONEY WOUNDS

I am healthy. I am wealthy. I am rich. I am that bitch.

—*Baby Tate*

I had two hand-me-down outfits in my closet when I started preschool in the mostly white California community of Laguna Niguel in the early eighties. One was a maroon tracksuit with white piping on the sides. The other was a pair of navy-blue Dickies-type pants and a red Lacoste shirt. After the first week of alternating between the two boyish-looking outfits and see-ing the other little girls in coordinated tops and bottoms with cute bows and socks to match, I begged and pleaded and pretty-pleased my mom to let me go to school wearing the light blue, ruffly, puffy-sleeved, quintessentially eighties dress she had recently bought me, but all I got was a stern stare and a hard no.

End of discussion. She still talks about how long she had to save for that costly party dress—too long for me to be dirtying it up on the playground, that's for sure. I often sense that she carries deep guilt over purchasing such an expensive dress for a rare occasion, but we've never talked about it in such depth. What I inevitably believed from this moment forward was that nice things were meant to be experienced only on rare occasions—I was not worthy of everyday nice.

Crushed, the super-girly girl within me swallowed her pride and did as she was told. As the weeks passed, I learned to endure the pointing fingers from the other little kids who made fun of me for only having two outfits. I went about my business making friends and playing Duck Duck Goose until the day one of my closest friends dropped a truth bomb on me on the playground: "You're poor. That's why you don't have more clothes."

I had no idea I was poor. I knew the other kids had more outfits than me, but I thought everyone's mom turned their underwear inside out so they could wear the same pair two days in a row. I didn't know that our apartment with the brown shag carpet and linoleum kitchen floors fell under California's low-income housing umbrella. My family had tacos de papa on the regular, but I didn't realize that my mom had only seven dollars a month to cover our basic needs, including food. Even beans were out of the question because the amount of frijoles it would take to feed us over a month cost more than a sack of potatoes, but I didn't know any better. Once again, we had different food only on special occasions, like when my uncle and aunts would come over with Chinese takeout, and I devoured every last bite with gusto. Other than asking to wear that dress, I never complained again about what we didn't have. I never wanted to make my mom feel bad.

But that day at school, I felt like Neo awakening to the Matrix, to a stark, alternate reality that I had been completely unaware of. Just recalling this memory constricts my heart and floods my eyes with tears. I suddenly understood that I was different from the kids around me. Yet I also felt sorrier for my parents than for myself. They were the ones struggling to feed us, and I perceived early on that I could either create more problems or ease their burdens. I chose the latter. I decided to keep quiet and stay under the radar as much as possible. I learned to be grateful for the little things, like family visits. My aunts and uncle always brought me toys. And my uncle usually slipped a ten-dollar bill in my pocket, which I would always give to my mom later. She still gets emotional recalling this, because that cash was "una bendición de Dios," heaven-sent in her eyes. She'd use it to buy more milk for me, which she'd then cut down with water to stretch it out—I guzzled it like a thirsty little calf.

Now, as an adult, I finally get it: the root of my money wounds—the scarcity, the anxiety triggered by living in constant survival mode, the shame of being called poor and laughed at for not having enough—began right there, at home. And it was just the tip of the iceberg.

Money wounds are mental and emotional barriers that limit our right to feel deserving of stability and wealth. Money wounds elicit emotions like fear, anxiety, shame, and guilt around the lack or abundance of money. Unlike physical wounds, our individual money wounds—and how they dictate our day-to-day decisions—are challenging to identify. Many of us don't even know we're functioning with them.

When we think about making money, most of us can't help but link it to sacrifice. We start a side hustle, stop eating out, work overtime. We're used to cutting out all enjoyment in order to scrimp and save, but doing so only digs us deeper into our money wounds, putting generational wealth further beyond our reach. Yet what many of us don't know is that money is in abundance and the ability to generate wealth already lives within us. Yes, it's right there, but getting to that destination in our journey will require patience, discipline, and compassion for ourselves, because confronting those wounds head-on is one of the hardest battles we will face on this wealth-building journey. It will get heavy, it will feel messy, it will be tough to stomach, but in order to get to the light, we must move through the darkness.

It took me more than thirty years to brave my money wounds. I had to become a warrior in my own life, hunting the emotions that run deep within my soul, digging so profoundly into my thoughts, my community, my past, that at times I felt it would swallow me whole. It was like walking into a murky, fog-laden cave unarmed, driven solely by the knowledge that on the other side were the weapons I needed to fight the oncoming internal and external battles on my Wealth Warrior path.

As you uncover your own wounds, the fog will begin to lift, and you will gain clarity on the emotions that have been holding you back financially. You will begin to feel more confident and empowered to disrupt this menacing cycle and jump-start your healing process. You will begin to base your money moves on empirical truths rather than feverish emotions. And eventually you will be able to leave the battlefield and return home to tend to your financial garden, planting wealth seeds and monitoring the weeds, replacing warlike emotional upheavals with peace of mind in your investment journey.

In order to get to the other side, to that place where investing is part of your weekly routine rather than something you dread and fear, you must first plant yourself firmly on the ground and face two combat zones: the keepers of your belief system and your predominant false beliefs. Slap on your war paint and get ready to start your emotional boot camp.

## FACE THE KEEPERS OF OUR BELIEF SYSTEMS

Where do our personal limitations come from? Many of our wounds begin with the false beliefs that work in favor of the economic system. These narratives have devout keepers: the privileged few in our society who have access to financial literacy, and even our own communities when we internalize the narratives used to keep communities of color suppressed. The keepers are self-aware; they understand how to benefit from the steadfast mass beliefs about finances that have been in place for years on end. They uphold the systemic and institutional barriers we face on the daily that keep us financially distant from the controlled environment that serves them, under the guise of keeping us "safe." In turn, we begin to fear what we may find on the other side of the fort we've created to stave off danger. Yet remaining in that fort believing our enemies only lurk at the perimeter also means we will likely remain struggling, fearful, impoverished, and unable to explore anything beyond those walls. Outside the fort is where investment opportunities live, where wealth is being generated, where abundance thrives. Our goal is to break free from the confinement of the fort and its keepers and join the land of wealth that is waiting for us.

But our battle doesn't stop there. We also have to pay attention to our more intimate circle—our community, our teachers, our friends, our family, our parents—the pillars who uphold this greater system of false beliefs and limitations within our own environment. These are the keepers who have raised us, the ones we trust the most to keep us safe. And they're also the ones who pass down some generational beliefs that may do more harm than good when it comes to money: *I have to work hard for money. I'm not good with money. Wealthy people are greedy. Money is the root of all evil.* As we move through life, we grow up desperately needing money yet totally fearing it. We need to let go of these self-imposed limitations, but it's incredibly difficult to generate a new personal belief when there's such a strong system in place that has been unknowingly passing on money wounds from one generation to the next. These limitations and wounds become a part of our own narrative as we grow up, and with time, we will continue to perpetuate them if we don't manage to wake the fuck up.

These beliefs are the wall that keeps us from leaving the fort. They're what keeps us from wealth-building opportunities that will help us construct the life of our dreams. That's why this is the most crucial part of our wealth-building journey. We can't reach the money-generating financial garden without attacking the fort and dismantling these constructs.

## REFRAME YOUR FALSE BELIEFS

The power you need to liberate yourself from your money wounds is currently blurred by your own set of false beliefs. These little fuckers are holding you hostage from the wealth you deserve, and you might not even be aware of them yet. In the following pages, I am going to explore the four most common false beliefs that continuously come up in our community and with my clients and students when we talk money. But, parallel to this, I also want you to start digging deep within yourself to begin identifying your own false beliefs, which may or may not coincide with the ones mentioned in these pages. Use the following exploration as a tool to apply to your own money wounds so you can begin to leave behind your limitations and reframe your mindset. I want us to reach a space where we no longer internalize our circumstances and instead embody our full, compassionate, and powerful Wealth Warrior potential.

*False Belief #1: I have to work hard for money.*

Every afternoon when the preschool bell rang, signaling the end of the day, I'd head outside and begin my one-block journey home alone, passing parents and other relatives picking up my classmates. When I reached our apartment door, I'd firmly grab the gold key hanging from the dirty white shoestring around my neck, unlock the door, and quickly shut it behind me, heart racing loud enough to break the eerie silence of that empty apartment. I had strict instructions from my mom: "Don't open the door or let anyone in." Classic latchkey-kid rules.

Once the door was secured, I headed straight to the kitchen for a bowl of cereal. I had to push a chair next to the counter and climb onto it to reach the off-brand cereal box in the cupboard. As I carefully poured the watered-down milk into my bowl, I could hear my mom's voice in my head: *Don't make a mess.* A while later, my mom would burst into the apartment, returning from her cleaning or babysitting job to rush to the kitchen and frantically start making a big batch of meat tacos. As soon as she finished frying them up, she'd place them in a big dish. "Ándale, mija," she'd say, and we'd head over to the fábrica to sell the freshly made food to the workers during the dinner break of their night shift on the line assembling circuit boards that would eventually be used for sprinkler systems. Just the smell of those crispy tacos turned my stomach into a growling monster, but I knew that this food was for us to sell, not for me to consume. I was very quiet, obedient, and empathetic toward my mom and our circumstances, so I went along with whatever she asked me to do back then—my outspoken side would flourish a few years later. Sometimes, when my mom offloaded enough tacos to make ends meet, she'd relax her rule and hand one over to me, which I'd devour with enormous pleasure. When the crowd started to fizzle, she'd pack up the big dish, drive back home in a flash, drop me off with my dad, who was back home from work by then, and head out for her graveyard shift at that same factory.

Many of us grew up seeing our parents and grandparents putting in long work hours and extreme physical labor to generate money. It was my model growing up too, as my mother's unofficial sous-chef, vacuumer, and babysitter once my little sister arrived four years after me. There was an understanding that life was sacrificed in exchange for money. Holidays were skipped because my mom was hired to serve dinners and clean up during and after family gatherings. It was the price we paid as a family to live in this country. We had to work hard for the money; we didn't know any other way.

Twenty-something years later, I embarked on my career at a TV station in Dallas, which required me to spend the majority of my time driving under the blazing Texas sun in a car with a broken AC. I was an account executive at the TV network Azteca América, cold-calling businesses and selling airtime to land accounts, and had to drive across the city to meet with execs we wanted to work with to expand our reach. Every day, I'd lodge paper towels under my armpits while driving and doing prep work to avoid the dreaded sweat circles from staining my top before the next high-powered meeting. This type of physical toll and strenuous, stressful work somehow made me feel like I was doing a great job and experiencing massive achievement. Sure, I was hot and couldn't afford to fix the AC, but I had to work only one job to make ends meet, versus the three to four jobs my mom worked. Yet there was always a little voice inside me that said, *You deserve more.*

That voice always filled me with instant guilt and shame. How could I possibly feel unhappy or want anything better for myself if I'd already gotten so much further than my own parents? I wasn't working in a factory or selling tacos or cleaning houses. And if those emotions didn't hit me quick enough, even daring to utter a subtle under-the-breath complaint to my mom after a long and clammy day at work would provoke a now classic speech from her: "I crossed the border by foot under the blazing sun for three straight days. Do you think I had AC while doing that? At least you have a car—when I got here, I had to take the bus without knowing how to get where I needed to go, because I couldn't speak English. You don't know the first thing about sacrifice, mija. Instead of whining about not being happy or being too hot, put your head down and just do the work." And that's what I did, janky AC and all.

I know you feel me. Maybe a similar scene has played out in your life too. Past generations of our families had to endure physical labor to make ends meet, and now we pour our all into desk jobs to climb the ladder, or hold down a few gigs at a time to do basic things like make rent or put away some savings. We spend boatloads of cash and get deep in student loan debt for an education that so many of us are not aligned with, which leads to working in a field we don't like, because it will make our parents proud. We forgo our true calling for old-fashioned hard work because we don't see a path to make money in easier, more efficient ways. But is money really worth sacrificing our physical, emotional, and spiritual well-being?

*Wealth Warrior Truth: Money works hard for me.*

When you spend a lifetime working hard for the money, you become emotionally attached to it, but guess what? Money ain't shit without you. You know who's the shit, the badass? You! Money doesn't happen unless you make it happen. It's the effect, and *you* are the cause. You are more important than money. If you want to build real wealth, you must learn how to let money go and deploy it in moneymaking investments so your job is not the be-all, end-all of your wealth-building journey. You may be thinking, *Wait, is that even possible?* Hell yeah!

Rather than something we contemplate and fear, investing should be a standardized experience. Investing is simply the action of putting money to work for you, versus you exchanging your time and energy for money. It is multiplying the money you make so that you can have freedom of choice in the future. Investing shouldn't require bravery, but it does because even though there's a free market out there, this concept is foreign to people of color who have had limited or no access to the resources that teach us how money works on a larger economic front. So investing immediately feels beyond our reach. This isn't entirely our fault. The world that we live in often requires us to meet our immediate needs first, keeping us in a cycle of working and spending. It also skips out on educating those of us who are not keepers of the system on financial tools we could use to succeed, particularly the stock market. This makes it a fight to not only understand how to generate wealth through investing, but once and for all break from the idea that we have to work extra hard for our money. So it's up to us to take the first steps to become Wealth Warriors.

To transform the belief that you have to work hard for money, you must jump into your investment journey. It's the best teacher. When your money begins to grow on its own in the stock market, your outlook on money will forever be changed because you will finally realize that money isn't solely dependent on you making it. It is dependent on you growing it.

We need to change our attitudes toward investing for ourselves, our families, and the generations to come so that we can begin to build the wealth we deserve without having to put our well-being in jeopardy in the process. This shift starts now.

Sacrifice for your dream, not for money. Every time I go in that direction, where I'm not promised anything, money always happens. It comes through. Because money is in abundance. There is no set amount of money that you are allowed to tap into. Only you have the power to impact how much dinero you make.

### False Belief #2: I'm not good with money.

For years, I felt that as soon as I received money, it would disappear. I couldn't amass it. I used to say, "I'm not good with money," and I fervently believed this to be true. There were times when the last few days before my next paycheck equaled a popping-open-a-can-of-beans-for-dinner type of struggle—but always dressed up with a little onion, cilantro, tomato, and fresh serranos. And then, when I landed my first well-paying job, at a furniture store, making $60,000 a year—which was a *huge* deal for me at twenty-four—I used that money to build my closet instead of my financial portfolio. I now had the money I so badly craved and needed, but my spending habits continued to nourish my false belief of not being good with money. In hindsight, that belief was a cop-out. It was part of my victim mentality: *These things are happening to me because I'm not good with money.* Those thoughts only justified my anxiety-driven habits and allowed me to avoid the topic entirely. Talk about a bullshit excuse. I didn't know it then, but it wasn't that my habits were *poor*; it was that they were *uninformed*. We can often get hung up on not being good at something without realizing that we just don't know how to do it.

The switch finally flipped for me one afternoon while I was watching an episode of *Oprah*, who was like my personal therapist back then—her words of wisdom got me through many dark times. She came on-screen and presented a book, Rhonda Byrne's *The Secret*, that awakened me to a new reality, one where our thoughts are one with the law of attraction. Something clicked. I understood right then and there that an emotional component and a belief system were blocking me from the knowledge and energy I needed to realize my dreams. After the credits rolled, I turned off the TV, glanced at my closet full of fresh clothes, and understood that although I had gone to business school, I had been so busy working and surviving that I hadn't really grasped the concepts I needed to make the kind of progress I dreamed of, like eventually making six figures and buying a home. That was when I became obsessed with figuring out how to generate more money.

There was a whole wealth of knowledge (no pun intended) about money that I didn't even know about—knowledge that would allow me to wield my money with power and never eat a can of beans for dinner again. So I set out on a quest to align my dreams with my everyday actions. I began to devour as many of the great financial literacy books as I could get my hands on. I became obsessed with old-school Wall Street men who were at the helm of incredibly successful corporations, because I felt they were my only option to experience and generate what was otherwise never modeled for or accessible to me. They were the only ones I saw amassing wealth like nobody's business. They were the cream of the crop—fast-talking in crisp suits, with coiffed hair, a wife, two kids, and trust funds to match. Moreover, on TV, in movies, and on the news, they were always depicted with a sense of ease. They laughed easily, smiled easily, and found easy solutions to their problems. I wanted to learn how to build a legacy and achieve that same level of effortlessness, which seemed out of reach despite the fact that I was making more than I ever had. So I sought out their knowledge to definitively change the belief that I was not good with money.

*Wealth Warrior Truth: I am more than capable of understanding money.*

The world of finance literature felt like a secret society. I could practically envision all these old Wall Streeters leaving work back in the 1800s in their crisp, high-collared shirts, vests, and dark tailored suits, then gathering in a dimly lit room, donning cloaks, holding white candles, whispering ancient financial wisdom to one another. I burned through their books but struggled to process the information. It was like reading code. All the talk of exchanges, stock charts, margins, corrections, bear and bull markets, made my head spin. I had to Google the meaning of every other word. I didn't know of anyone else with this information, and I already felt generations behind.

So I pushed myself because I knew that eventually my relentless work would allow me to start making sense of this cryptic financial literature. Yet despite building my arsenal of knowledge and information on money, I still felt that the key to breaking through my "I'm not good with money" belief was working harder—reading more books by more people whose life experiences did not match mine, because I found no others to turn to. I remember having a moment when I glanced at my stack of books and thought, *Shit, they're all written by white men.* Well, it is their system, after all. How could I expect to find a treasure trove of books by people of color talking money when financial literacy is inaccessible by design? Instead of courses that nurture kids' natural desire to follow their curiosity and build something, or even better, a clear financial literacy curriculum, most kids in US public schools receive instructions, perform certain tasks, and are measured by these tasks. This makes for great employees but ultimately keeps us from wealth-generating mindsets. We all know the story of people who are stellar workers but wake up decades later infuriated and regretful because they were trained to help others in their wealth-building journeys rather than embark on their own.

Thankfully, the tides are turning, and there are many creative ways to make money. But the foundation of wealth is knowledge. A basic understanding of economics is a complete game changer that has the power to lead you to massive growth. A true Wealth Warrior takes it to the next level by understanding how to tap into new ways of generating wealth and making that wealth work for them. Don't expect to become an expert overnight—it's a process, but it's worth every minute of the precious time you put into it. We must shrewdly fight the knowledge keepers with knowledge of our own: become proficient in this secret language, master the system, and at long last tap into this wealth-generating movement and start calling it our own.

### False Belief #3: Wealthy people are greedy.

One of the most common beliefs that I have seen surface in our communities of color time and again throughout my life is that wealthy people are greedy. Oftentimes, the word *wealth* conjures images of white men and their families who—despite living in enormous mansions on acres of land, with lavish spreads of food on the dinner table, and walk-in closets brimming with unused clothes—want more, more, more. With this pervasive image in mind, wealth is an experience that we grow up believing is way beyond our reach. What's more, the mere idea of striving for a position in life that is usually filled by the keepers of the system who have hurt our communities of color, the ones we are trying to battle, feels incredibly challenging and counterintuitive. On a subconscious level, we can't help but start to think that if we dare to amass any amount of wealth, it will immediately make us as greedy as those who have oppressed us. It's as if wealth holds such power over us that having it will automatically make us bad people with bad motives who gain wealth through bad practices. So when we earn some extra cash that enables us to improve our life in some way—like buying a new car with a working AC—we go out of our way to try to downplay it.

Back in the eighties, after a few years of working several jobs day and night and running an extra-tight ship at home by serving tacos de papa for dinner, my mom managed to scrimp and save enough money for a down payment on an affordable condo in San Juan Capistrano, California. Although my parents, little sister, and I lived in scarcity, my mom actively taught me how to build generational wealth. She had the audacity to break from what was expected of someone who cleans houses, works at a factory, and speaks broken English. She aspired to something outside her current circumstances, which allowed her to buy a home that is still in our family today and is worth ten times what she paid for it back then.

When we moved into the two-bedroom condo, I felt a clear shift in our lifestyle. Long gone were the days of two hand-me-down outfits in my closet. Now we could actually afford to go to the swap meet to buy some new clothes. Instead of playing underneath a stairwell, I was hanging out at the public horse stables across the street. That place became my backyard. I'd come home from school, drop my backpack, and beeline it over to the stables to see the horses and watch the people ride. Just beyond the stables was a network of creeks framed by scenic, verdant hills that my six-year-old eyes interpreted as majestic mountains. I'd get lost looking at that view and daydream about what I'd find if I ever made it to the other side of those hills.

But when I returned home, if I mentioned the stables one too many times or gushed about my new clothes, my mom would immediately fall into scolding mode and launch into a lecture about acting like we were better off than others. She urged me to not flaunt it so openly, or else we'd be seen as crass and insensitive. Instead, she pushed me to act poorer than we were. My mom explicitly told me to never discuss that we owned the condo. It was best to allow people to assume we rented. I was to never share that my mom was actually flourishing with her housekeeping business and bringing in more money now. When my dad bought a new car, she reacted like it was the worst thing he could've done to her. The strange thing was that she actually began to purchase nice furniture and picked up a great sense of style from all the houses she cleaned. So we could enjoy some luxuries behind closed doors, but out in public we had to act like we didn't have much to our name. Suddenly, acquiring any sort of wealth, even in small amounts, began to feel shameful. I went from relishing and celebrating our new lifestyle to believing that having money made me bad and unlikable. The last thing I wanted was for people to think we were greedy. The internal conflict gave me whiplash. Years later, when I was driving my first decent car in my neighborhood and caught sight of the paletero on the corner, I felt embarrassed about having a nice ride. God forbid my family get lumped into that wealthy-greedy category.

By accepting the subconscious belief that wealth makes us

greedy, we stop ourselves from growing and amassing money and close ourselves off to the very experience of wealth. We accept smaller salaries, say no to good opportunities, lose faith in our dreams, push investing to the back of our minds, and neglect the moneymaking tools that will secure our future. Up until a few years ago, I focused on making only enough to survive. I didn't need more, because needing or wanting more was greedy, wanting more took away from others, and wanting more led to taking the easy road in life, diminishing all the hard work and sacrifice, and I was better than that—my mom is probably nodding emphatically after reading this sentence.

I carried this belief so steadfastly that while at Azteca América, when I was approached by Liberman Broadcasting with an $80,000-a-year job offer, which was double what I was making at the time, I immediately declined. I knew a little about the station, particularly that *some* of their content proliferated the stereotype of hypersexual Latinas by making us look hot and clueless on-air. It's not that I was against being sexy. After being made fun of for having only two outfits in kindergarten, I developed a deep desire to express myself through clothes and fun accessories. I just saw myself in more dynamic characters who were both sexy *and* smart, like in my projects at Azteca América. So I didn't take the meeting. I didn't ask more questions. I didn't consider how that bump in my salary would allow me to fix my car's busted AC unit so I would no longer have to drive in the Texas heat with all four windows rolled down in a tornado of debris, hair, and highway noise. I just said no. The temptation to consider such money alone made me feel like I could immediately succumb to the greediness I had spent years avoiding by making safe, tactical career decisions. Yet by allowing this belief to intervene, my righteousness blocked an opportunity that could've upgraded my quality of life—turns out Liberman had multiple stations, and not all featured this reductive content I was all up in arms about.

*Wealth Warrior Truth: Wealth gives me options.*

The keepers of our belief system within our inner circle—a.k.a. our close friends and family, those whom we interact with on a daily basis—have such a strong hold on us, they can easily influence our day-to-day actions and determine the directions of our lives. In the same way, we can influence their actions too—let's not fool ourselves; we participate in this system too, even if to a lesser degree. Challenging this belief system is often punishing in the moment because you run the risk of suffering personal attacks and rupturing close relationships. *¿Quién se cree? Se cree mucho. Who does she think she is? Ah, so you think you're all that now that you've left the hood. You think you're better than us because you have more money?* How many times have we received or given this type of wounding judgment?

As soon as we begin to teach our own lineage this system of false beliefs, we are transferring our inherited money wounds to the next generation. And in doing so, we continue to adhere to and uphold the system that is keeping us suppressed. We begin to judge others—in person, online, or even quietly in our own heads—for having money, for making more of it, for amassing it, and especially for spending it. *How can they afford that nice* car? *What a show-off! I can't believe they bought that brand-name bag instead of saving money for an emergency—how wasteful!* These are the thoughts masking the fact that we reject the idea of luxury because we feel shame that it's out of reach. Maybe your vacation fund isn't quite there yet, or your income doesn't allow for the latest self-care craze. There's that scarcity mindset again! It's important to pause for a moment and think, *What wound is my judgment masking? Who is the keeper of this belief that associates greed with wealth? Why am I upholding it? How is this belief affecting my choices around money? How is it restricting me from thinking bigger? Most importantly, what are the ways in which I am already wealthy?*

To be clear, I'm not asking you to leave your community. I want you to break free from this particular belief that associates wealth with greed, so that you can have the freedom to create and choose your own wealth-building options (we'll get to those in the next chapter). Once you gain the knowledge and the tools, you'll be able to share and spread them throughout your family and community and continue breaking this cycle that has been holding us all back from true financial safety and security for so long.

Ironically enough, many of our keepers—our parents and grandparents—broke cycles themselves. When they decided to immigrate to this country—whether by choice or through need—they broke free from their own systems in search of a more bountiful garden. Our ancestors are the real trailblazers in our lineage. My mom and one of her brothers were the first to leave Mexico in search of growth and opportunity to help their family back home. Once they started working in the United States, every single paycheck—after bills and rent for their shared housing were paid—went straight to my grandparents. With that money, my grandparents were able to go from barely making ends meet to buying land, cattle, pigs, and chickens, and even building a nicer house. My mom and uncle were crucial to building generational wealth in our family. Most of their twelve siblings followed their lead. There was definite judgment from those who stayed behind in their community, maybe some envy and sadness in the mix too, but the fruits of their labor are still being consumed to this day. Their search for a "better" life by no means guaranteed an easy one—they went through a massive uprooting with nothing in front of them except pure faith. And yes, some part of their motivation for doing this was, in fact, wealth, if not for themselves, then for their parents and children. Gasp!

At the end of the day, wealth doesn't make us *greedy*; it gives us *options*. When my mom was able to save up enough money, she chose to buy a condo. She wouldn't have had that option had she not amassed her hard-earned wealth. In turn, instead of focusing on the cycle that kept us poor until that point, I use my wealth-generating investments to provide for my family. It's given me the freedom to choose what's best for me and my loved ones. So nowadays, when my mom calls me and says, "Ay, mija, why are you so terca about becoming a millionaire? ¿Para qué quieres más?" attempting to resuscitate the greediness belief, instead of spiraling into self-doubt and wondering if my desire for wealth does in fact make me greedy, I can now laugh it off.

When you face your own wealth-building fears and false

beliefs, remember this: the word *wealthy* belongs to us too. According to the *New World Encyclopedia*, the root of the word *wealth* is *well-being*. Our well-being and that of the collective shouldn't sit in the same space as greed in our minds. We can do so much more for our community when we are wealthy. Wealth gives us options. It gives us choices. I can't tell you how satisfying it is for me when I buy products or services curated by people who reflect me and embody the first-generation American culture I was raised in. This is something I can do with my money; it's one of my options, and I choose to support us. We are limitless and deserving of everything we strive for.

### False Belief #4: Money is the root of all evil.

"For the love of money is the root of all evil." Every time I hear this famous Bible verse, I'm pulled back to younger me pounding my heart alongside the rest of the congregation, saying, "Por mi culpa, por mi gran culpa." With that gesture, I learned to punish my truth, punish my potential, punish my essence. Yet at the end of the sermon, without fail, we were urged to drop our *evil* dollars in the small woven basket being passed around in the house of God.

The false belief that money is the root of all evil has been upheld for so long, it has transcended church and infected the masses from generation to generation. This is one of the most dangerous false beliefs we carry with us and another hard one to shatter because it can feel so conflicting. Many of us grow up hating money because we believe it is the evil that is holding us back, or it's the evil that caused a rift in our family, or it's the evil that pushed us into the abyss of poverty. Yet money is pivotal to our survival, to paying our debts and dues, to securing housing, to staying fed.

If money is the root of all evil, then what the hell are we doing working forty-plus hours a week throughout most of our lives to obtain this evil? So we need evil to survive? Take a moment to process this. Now visualize the battle happening between your conscious and subconscious. If your subconscious believes you are generating an abundance of evil just by making money, you can imagine the ginormous challenge you will face when trying to consciously generate an abundance of wealth. All along we've been hating the very *tool* we need not just to survive but to thrive.

*Wealth Warrior Truth: Money is a tool. It is not part of my soul or my character.*

Money is not an evil monster; it's not an emotion; it's not our ruler. Money is currency, a tool we use in exchange for goods and services. A tool we need to pay for rent, expenses, food, and clothes. Take a dollar bill from your wallet. Touch it, look at it, flip it around. You are basically holding a piece of paper in your hand that is no longer even backed by the gold standard—a monetary system where the value of a country's currency is directly linked to the value of gold. Now it's printed as needed by the Fed. So, in a sense, it has no real value—it is worthless. I know this may sound insensitive because we're used to putting so much power in money and we've become so dependent on where it comes from, but by doing so, we are minimizing our own personal power. Your circumstances have likely created barriers in your life, but nobody can take away your power, because nothing is more valuable than you. Money is just a tool we need to survive in this world. That's it. And there's nothing wrong with wanting to obtain a shit ton of it to distribute in ways that *WE* see fit.

During a trip to California around a year or so after I first was approached by Azteca América's competitor, I received a phone call. It was Liberman Broadcasting, the media company that had tried to tempt me with an $80,000 salary a year earlier, which I had vehemently declined. But since that initial offer, I had been on a road to discovering what it felt like to be supported by my power. I wasn't chasing money; I was focused on me, on my healing, on building my own inner strength, and I intuitively knew that by doing so, the money would soon follow. And I began to trust myself when it did. That was the start of a major mindset shift in my life. So this time, I took the call. "Hey, we heard you're in LA. We'd like to talk to you while you're in town." I said yes to the interview and they offered me a position on the spot at a radio station in Orange County that played Spanish-language oldies—no demeaning depictions of Latinas in sight. And now I was able to check my false beliefs at the door. I couldn't let my money wounds stop me from making one of the best decisions of my life—so I took the job. In hindsight, that bump in salary was a pebble-sized stepping-stone toward the lifestyle I aspired to have one day. The first thing I did was head to the nearest department store to buy a stash of new underwear, a tradition of sorts I began as soon as I started making money as an adult. I always have a new pair ready to wear. But what this job really did was encourage me to take bigger risks to achieve my goals.

I honestly didn't see money as a tool just yet, but I was finally able to let go of the idea that I had to do something I hated to make money. It was the first time money didn't hold such extensive power over me, and I liked it. Less than a year later, I decided to leave that big salary behind to take the next step toward my dream: working in Hollywood.

The only way to get my foot in the door at a movie studio was through an unpaid internship. So I fired off résumés and got a call from After Dark Films, a company that produced horror movies. The summer intern position was mine, and I took the biggest leap of faith of my life and said yes. In what felt like a mere heartbeat, I had gone from an account executive making eighty grand a year to a thirty-year-old unpaid intern dealing with eviction notices because I no longer had the money to pay my rent. But I tightly grasped the handlebar during this rollercoaster period of my life because my gut knew that this experience would eventually pay off.

Imagine if we all discovered right now how powerful we really are and that we don't *have to* labor for our money or for someone else's goals. Imagine if we could tap into our personal power instead of giving it all away to the money we *don't* have—it would be a total game changer. By giving money less power, I was able to release myself from its stranglehold, tap into my personal power, quit the job that no longer made me happy, and dare to go for what would. And by reframing our false beliefs, we now have the potential to kick the fear of building wealth and investing, and finally enter the battlefield with the weapons necessary to win this fight.

## LET THE HEALING BEGIN

Now that you are starting to identify your own money wounds and are becoming aware of the false beliefs that inform your life, decisions, and mindset; now that you have identified the keepers of this system, I want to share with you three Wealth Warrior missions that will get you started on your wealth-generating journey. Commit to at least one of them. If you find that your money wounds and false beliefs are activated, remain steadfast. Go back to our Wealth Warrior Truths to ground yourself in abundance and remind money who's in charge. After all, scared money don't make money.

### Find Your Money-Conscious Fam

The first time I told my mom I had money in the stock market, after three years of investing, she frantically replied, "Mija, you need to take it out of there immediately! You can't leave it in there. You could lose everything!" To her, my hard-earned cash was exiting my hands and disappearing into some nebulous, inaccessible space: "in there." By then, I had started to open up about money with others in my community who knew about finances, yet when I mentioned the stock market, I was surprised to receive the same response. The message? *Work with the money you have because the stock market is not meant to work for you.* My false belief flag was going all the way up, so I took a step back, realigned my thoughts, and decided it was time for some money-wound maintenance with my money-conscious family: Bricia and Patty.

I met Bricia in Los Angeles at an awards ceremony for *Latino Leaders*, a national magazine headquartered in Dallas. At that time, my career was finally beginning to take shape—I'd gone from unpaid intern to marketing coordinator at Lionsgate's Pantelion Films, the first major Latine Hollywood movie studio, joining a trailblazing team that was carving out space for Latines in the industry. *Latino Leaders* had selected me for their Leaders of the Future award for all the work I was doing to raise awareness on social media about Latine content, backed by research that showcased why we needed to start watching and paying attention to it. Back when I was sweating through my shirts in my car with no AC, I had once said to myself, *One day I will be featured in this magazine*, and now that moment had finally arrived. Thrilled, I got all dolled up and headed to the ceremony. After settling in at my assigned table, I quickly struck up a conversation with the woman next to me, Bricia, a Oaxacan-American restaurateur, and co-owner of one of the most famous Oaxacan restaurants in Los Angeles. She's a tough broad with a kind heart. I loved her no-nonsense, tell-it-like-it-is attitude and unapologetic hunger for growth—traits that spoke to my heart. By the end of the night we'd exchanged numbers, and the following week we were already texting like we'd been besties all along. As I got to know her better, I realized our lives couldn't be more different. Her family is likely the closest-knit one I have ever met—both her parents were present when she was growing up and they raised their kids to work toward common goals. I never had that, but I yearned to take a page from her book and build a close working relationship with my own family in which each member's personal goals were supported collectively, so her perspective was invaluable to me.

A while after we began to forge our friendship, Bricia invited me to A Taste of Mexico, one of the events she produced. That evening, while schmoozing with the crowd, she tapped my shoulder and said, "Linda, I want you to meet my friend Patty." The second I heard Patty's voice, my heart stopped.

Every Wednesday, while on my two-hour drive trudging through LA's rush-hour traffic from my shared apartment in Santa Ana to my internship at After Dark Films, I'd listen to *On Air with Ryan Seacrest*, more specifically to a Latina who had a regular segment on that day. With her distinct Latina accent, she made me feel at home, as if I were on the phone with one of my friends, talking about the latest trends and giving advice. I felt like I had known her all my life, my new morning-drive bestie.

"Patty Rodriguez?" I asked, immediately fangirling.

She smiled and nodded. Patty is a nationally recognized entrepreneur, media personality, radio producer, bestselling author, and angel investor in Latine startups—she is the reason why Selena has a MAC cosmetics collection. She's also the most fearless woman I have ever met. She wears her heart on her sleeve and turns the emotions conjured by the injustices she observes into action, leveraging her platform at all costs to do right by her community. Patty is not after the glory that comes with her selfless feats, she's after real change.

From that moment onward, the three of us became inseparable. Pursuing our dreams kept us so busy we didn't have much spare time to meet up in person, but there wasn't a day that went by without at least a few texts buzzing back and forth in our group chat. It was a very intimate relationship, one I'd never experienced before. We chatted about business moves, books, and the amount of wealth we wanted to amass.

Our money talks started with something a little less tangible—our dreams. "I want to write a book," said Bricia one day. Inspired by her forthrightness, I replied, "I want to make movies." And Patty added, "I want to have a publishing company." We quickly realized this was a safe space where we could openly voice our true desires and most outlandish dreams. The key was bringing these dreams back to reality and getting down to business to make them come true.

Bricia led the conversation. Her parents had made it a point to teach her about business and how to be a boss from a young age, which was rare in communities of color. They now have one of the most successful restaurants in Los Angeles and a James Beard Award to their name. I felt every win that Bricia and her family accomplished was my win too—she set an example of what was possible for us and made it okay to dream really, really big. We need an army of Bricias in our communities! When it came to money, Bricia was up front and assertive and brought up the subject with ease in our chats.

Meanwhile, Patty and I had never had these types of honest conversations. We had to divest ourselves of the impulse to shy away from money talk, because we knew it to be crucial to our ambitions. So we perked up our ears and followed Bricia's lead, setting aside the false beliefs that had hounded us for years and creating space for these invaluable conversations. These two amazing women quickly became the founding members of my money-conscious family—the people I could openly talk to about money, my dreams, and wanting more, without judgment. On the contrary, we supported and pushed one another to not drop the ball on our visions. Wealth suddenly became a positive subject in my life, something I could and should strive for. Their insight demystified the worries that our parents had when we were growing up, so now I could approach the idea of making bank to build my dreams with confidence instead of fear. Most importantly, I could trust that my people would have my back and offer genuine guidance when I had silly questions or was tackling a big problem. It was a game changer for all of us.

Back then Patty and I were trying to get our cash off the ground beyond trading our time for a paycheck; we were aiming to make real money. Bricia already owned a successful restaurant but was striving for more growth. Now Bricia and Patty are both running multimillion-dollar businesses. They were by my side when I first dove into the stock market, listening to my fears, celebrating my wins, and supporting my journey. And after carefully observing how my investment was growing, they eventually gave it a shot too. That was when our talks shifted from general finance to stocks, following the evolution of our wealth-building journey. Bricia and Patty were my safe space, where I had room to grow and thrive without judgment, where I learned how to tackle my false beliefs and befriend the idea of wealth, and where I began to see money as a tool, as a means to an end rather than an enemy I had to conquer.

Find your money-conscious fam. We're out here. Look for that safe space that houses other people vibrating at the same frequency as you—like-minded people, folks with similar goals and values, people in the same place in life as you. These can be your academic peers, a trusted coworker, a longtime friend. Before you approach them, take inventory of their behaviors toward money to see who is in a scarcity mindset and who is in one of abundance. You need to make sure the space you enter is fertile ground—discussing your money moves on barren soil can create major setbacks in your progress. You may need to go beyond your circle to cultivate this type of mindset shift. The good news is that nowadays, you can find money-focused communities of color on social media—find a content creator with sound advice who communicates money matters in a way that makes sense to you. Chances are you will also resonate with the community that follows them. There are also groups that host online networking events, finance podcasts, and other resources within your reach, so take advantage of it all to create this safe space for you.

Money-conscious people don't necessarily have to be currently amassing large sums of cash, but, like you, they should be on a road to self-awareness, learning to place power in themselves rather than in money. Money-conscious people bet on themselves and then use money as a tool to make good on that bet. Bricia and her siblings bought their parents out of their already thriving business and took it to new heights, creating a michelada product that is now sold at Costco. And Patty cofounded the media company Sin Miedo Productions and made good on her dream by also cofounding Lil' Libros, a bilingual children's book publishing company. She's investing not only in her ideas, but in her community's imagination, helping them turn those thoughts into tangible pages and other media. Connecting with these types of like-minded individuals will help you find your footing and inspire confidence in your own journey. Only then will you be prepared to consciously enter other conversations about money, which may be more difficult to navigate.

Practicing how to openly and confidently talk about money and your investments with your family and friends—a big taboo in the Latine community—is the beginning of the crucial healing process. Enter these particular conversations consciously and with empathy. They will shed light on the wounds you carry and help you reinforce your new Wealth Warrior Truths.

If you're not sure how to begin, here are a few conversation starters:

✓ "I'm looking at ways to improve my credit score." Proceed to share your score or past credit mistakes you have made. This will create a vulnerable space primed for sharing. You can follow this up with "Have you worked on your credit score? Are you comfortable sharing it with me?"

✓ "I've been working on being aware of the thoughts I
have surrounding money, and I realized I have some
beliefs that go against what I want to accomplish."
This is a good way to start talking about false beliefs
and how they affect our wealth-building decisions.

✓ "I'm thinking about investing in the stock market.
Have you begun this journey or ever considered it?"
This one may be met with some defensiveness or fear
of the unknown, but try to listen to the other person's money wounds speaking and then explore that
fear together with a follow-up like "I know, it's super
scary, but there's an opportunity there that I think
may be worth exploring."

Prepare yourself for a range of reactions from family and
friends—keep in mind all the emotions that we've talked about
and how a money talk with a new person may activate fear,
defensiveness, or sadness. Have compassion for those who aren't
fully supportive of you. Rather than focusing on changing their
minds, take note of the emotions these conversations dredge up
in *you*. Those are *your* money wounds and false beliefs speaking,
the ones that still require your attention. And leave some room to
be surprised—you never know who may already have the stock
market on their mind.

If you feel you aren't yet prepared to have this type of conversation with the family and friends who act as keepers of your
belief system, then continue to honestly face your false beliefs
and money wounds within the safety of your money-conscious

family. They will help you identify the shadows you cannot see for yourself and provide a space for you to comfortably work through your limitations. Their support and your mutual curiosity will create a feeling of confidence as you set out on your Wealth Warrior journey. This is profound and complex work, so if you come across barriers or traumas that feel insurmountable, don't hesitate to reach out to a therapist or another mental health professional with whom you feel a connection, someone you believe will understand where you're coming from. Call out your emotions, draw the boundaries needed, and hold those lines for the person you are growing into. It's like cleaning your house. Let go of everything that is not serving you, make sure that everything that is serving you is accounted for, and be clear on how to access it. Then tap into it. Every single day.

## Put a Lid on the Pobrecita Yo and Step Out of Victimhood

I began to fully embody my Wealth Warrior status only a few years back, when I stopped acting like a perpetual victim at money's mercy. It's a pattern that began to take root in me as a latchkey kid living in low-income housing in California with only two outfits to my name. When we moved to the condo in San Juan Capistrano, things began to look up, and for a brief moment, I thought our life had changed for the better and for good. But this would turn out to be a short-lived interlude. My parents' relationship was in a downward spiral at the time. Mom had reached her limit with Dad, and she became very cold and disconnected.

Any little thing could spark an angry reaction, so my dad, my sister, and I began to walk on eggshells each time we were around her. I felt sorry for my dad—he'd finally started making really big changes in his life, like getting sober, but it seemed to be too little, too late in my mom's eyes. One day, she looked him dead in the eye and, with an eerily serene voice, said, "No te necesito. I want a divorce." Her mom and family insisted she stay the course, telling her that unhappiness came with the territory and that she was obliged to endure it under Catholic law. But Mom was not having it anymore. After years of working relentlessly to build up our lives while assimilating into American culture at a time when women were finally able to own their voice, she knew that she could provide for herself and her children—this allowed her to feel her value and tap into her power. She certainly wasn't going to accept such treatment on a formality. So she packed up our bags, said to my dad, "Stay here—we're leaving," and moved me and my little sister out of the condo and into a gated apartment complex in Laguna Hills. Gone were the creek and the hills of San Juan and with them my solace.

My mom's mental health quickly began to deteriorate, and her power as an independent and resourceful woman began to fade. Noticing the abrupt shift in her behavior, my dad, aunts, and uncles decided we should head over to Dallas so she could be closer to her family. We crashed with one of my uncles until my mom felt stable enough to find our own place. That's when my dad moved to Dallas and back in with us. Everything was starting to regain some semblance of normalcy until I woke up one morning to my mom calling the tenants who had rented the

San Juan Capistrano condo. "You have thirty days to leave," she said, and hung up the phone. Then she met my bewildered eyes and added, "Come on, mija, we're going back to California." She loaded me in the passenger seat and my little sister in the back, and we left my dad for good. I was around ten years old.

As soon as we moved back into our old condo, I immediately rushed outside to explore the creeks and magical hills in what I recalled as my vast playground. But things had changed. When I started fifth grade the now predominantly Latine neighborhood kids made fun of me for speaking like a white girl, which was the vocabulary and accent I had picked up in what used to be a mainly white school. Then they started pushing me around—"Do you think you're better than us?" It was the 1980s. School bullying was something you just had to deal with—the teachers didn't intervene, and neither did the parents. With no support to fall back on, I shrank into a corner. All I wanted to do was put together cool outfits, listen to music, come up with choreographies—I was far from a fighter. But the bullying continued escalating. For some reason, these kids had it in for me. By sixth grade, I was receiving death threats from my classmates and calls at home 24/7. It got so bad that we started leaving our landline off the hook. Fear began to invade my every waking minute. No matter where I was, I constantly glanced over my shoulder to see if I was being followed, not wanting to be taken by surprise if I was jumped.

And then it finally happened.

I was at the local public library, working on a school book report, when a black belt eighth grader, someone I didn't even know or recognize, cornered me in one of the aisles and said, "I heard you were talking shit about me." That phrase in our school was code for "I'm about to beat your ass." She absolutely destroyed me. It felt like she turned my face inside out. Her friends stood around in a circle and watched. It was so bad, the librarians actually jumped in and pulled her off me to stop the attack. I shakily stood up, grabbed my belongings, and stumbled home, bleeding, dizzy, with a throbbing pain in my head. When I walked through our doorway later that day, my mom took one look at me and said, "What did you do to deserve that?" I tried to explain how it had gone down, but she replied, "Pues, you must've done something to provoke her." End of subject. Zero compassion. A complete disconnection from reality.

I thought that fight would mark the end of my torture, but those kids were just getting started. When they found out where I lived, they began to run by and throw two-by-fours through our windows, shattering the glass into a million pieces. The two friends I had were so afraid to be seen with me, they began to avoid me at school—we hung out only behind closed doors at home. When another girl tried to fight me, I got home that day and told my mom, "I can't do this anymore." She finally decided to enroll me at another school, in Laguna Beach, but I didn't fit in there either. Learning became the last thing on my mind because all my energy was focused on surviving the next massive crisis in my life. I didn't feel loved at school or at home. I quietly sensed that my mom hated me, as if I had ruined her life in some way. Her attitude toward my sister was a different story. I saw first-hand the love and understanding I yearned for, so I knew she had it in her, but it was never directed my way. When I sought my mom's support or protection, I was met with rejection. So I started acting out and running away, staying at strangers' homes nearby, seeking anyone who would welcome me in. Finally, one day, I said to my mom, "I'm moving to Texas to live with Dad."

One month in, someone broke into my dad's apartment and stole his televisions. He became nervous about leaving me home alone, but I didn't see the problem. A stolen TV sounded much better than a swollen face, and I had a list of safety precautions committed to memory. Still, he couldn't handle it. "I can't take care of you." He moved me in with an aunt. I never lived with either of my parents again. A year later, I was thirteen and pregnant.

This type of trauma and inconsistency takes many forms, especially in communities of color and immigrant families. We have to start working at a young age to pull our weight at home because our siblings need us or because it's the cultural norm, especially for daughters. We have to consider alternative post-secondary options because college is not within our means. Slowly, without us even noticing, money, or the lack of it, starts to take hold of our lives and gains more power over us. It begins to dictate our decisions, leaving us with fewer and fewer resources, cutting us off from the valuable experiences we need to build stability and positive home environments. The thought of generational wealth couldn't be more far-fetched when there are so many daily problems to solve first.

Our environment becomes our mindset. Our mindset becomes our decisions. Our decisions become our stories. And soon, victimhood takes root, and our scarcity mentality replaces our dreams. We start putting our stories front and center on applications, in social media, and in our communities as an excuse for why we can't advance. *Pobrecita yo, I try so hard, but no matter what I do, I can't seem to catch a break.* The more we look for reasons we can't do something, the more we will find them, which in turn propels us to solidify our false belief system and create a never-ending cycle that we model to our family and friends and hand down to our children. It's a vicious circle that must end with us.

The pobrecita yo doesn't have the strength to get out of harm's way. When I set out to become an entrepreneur in my mid-thirties, I was creating events that provided a relaxing space for women, using rituals that were meant to heal specific traumas in our communities, but all the while, I was making just enough to break even. I wanted these women to tap into their power, but I wasn't doing that for myself. I didn't know my worth, and that prevented me from charging an adequate amount for my time and services. I could hear myself saying, "Don't worry, yo me las arreglo, I'll figure it out; that's the story of my life." That pobrecita yo victim mentality allowed me to receive only whatever could be handed down to me, like those two outfits I had to alternate during preschool. I didn't dare ask for more, because I saw other people as pobrecitas too. How could I charge them full price? What if they didn't have enough?

Misery loves company. Stating that you and everyone around you are poor or lacking in something sets an intention for yourself and your personal experience. Think back to the keepers of the system and try to find where this pobrecita yo mentality began for you. Think about how it impacted you as a child, your development. Then choose your words and actions with more intention. Instead of focusing on what is lacking, keep your eye on the wealth you want to achieve. Instead of spending endless time brooding about the past and the what-ifs that haunt you—what if my dad had given us child support, or my mom hadn't had to work three jobs to put food on the table, or I hadn't felt responsible for my family growing up and instead could've lived a carefree adolescence?—use that time to set your eyes on the future and start learning how to put money to work for you. The time has come to step into your Wealth Warrior power and claim your territory by beginning to break away from the generational money wounds and false beliefs that have held your family and community down. Like Jenny69 said in her song, it's time to go "from a pobrecita to a bad bitch."

## Rewire Your Brain

To rewire our behavior and our beliefs, we first need to rewire our brains on a neurological level. Yeah, I'm totally going to nerd out and get scientific on you. Bear with me—it's worth it.

The **reticular activating system (RAS)** is a collection of neurons located in the brain stem that receives input on everything that activates our senses. It can filter up to two million active data bits at a time and works with the brain to determine what is important and how we react to it. The RAS is responsible for filtering out noise to maintain sleep, our fight-or-flight response, and how we perceive the world, processing and reinforcing what is already in our subconscious. Based on its analysis, it feeds us the information we need in order to survive each moment of our lives.

For many of us who grew up in survival mode, the RAS has grown accustomed to being overstimulated. It has become way too used to responding in this extreme way when, for example, we run up a credit card or have a bill we can't pay that month. When we think about how we don't have enough money to cover that expense, our systems immediately kick into high gear and hyperfocus on the problem (*I can't pay this bill*) rather than the solution (*How can I pay this bill?*).

Your thoughts matter. They have a real effect on how your brain filters information that is valuable to you. And while we may not be able to control our thoughts, we have an incredible capacity to direct our attention to a specific place. This means we have the power to focus on either our false beliefs or our Wealth Warrior Truths. To get to this point of actively choosing the information you process, you will first need to rewire your brain.

Let's go back to *I can't pay this bill*. What emotions does this bring up? The first thing I feel is a pang of anxiety, followed by worry and fear. The thoughts that come up are *I don't feel supported and I can't support myself*, which awakens a sense of failure; *I should have it together by now*, which brings forth shame; and *What is wrong with me?* Here comes the anger, the guilt. The behavior that follows these thoughts and emotions is straight-up survival mode. We think, *I've been here before—I know how to get through this*, so the RAS focuses on getting enough money to survive this particular expense.

What happens next? We attract experiences we are hardwired to handle; it is how our minds have been conditioned. In terms of money, we attract the exact amount of money we need to survive. Nine hundred for rent, no more, no less. But it comes with such a sense of relief that we think this is a positive outcome, and we cement this behavior in our brains so that we can access it the next time we need to cope with a similar situation. What's more, we become addicted to this hero feeling, where we barely slide underneath the trapdoor just before it clamps down on the floor. It begins to curtail our ability to create a positive association with wealth, one that will have a long-term effect on our life.

So how can we rewire our brains? Instead of thinking, *I can't pay this bill*, try this: *I have used money to pay my bills many times. My heart is open to beginning to receive long before my bills are due.*

*It is safe to have more money than what is needed.*

Repeat it a few times: *It is safe to have more money than what is needed.* Bonus points if you say this in the mirror so you can see yourself too. The sound of your voice speaking highly of your relationship to money will get your RAS working on this new, high-vibrational stimulus, triggering it to pick up on new solutions to seemingly impossible problems. This will become evidence of your new thought pattern, it'll help you change the narrative, and it'll open you up to seeing this entire experience from a completely different perspective.

My go-to memory is Christmas Eve—which for Latines is more important than Christmas Day. I was fresh out of college, struggling to find work in media and living in a one-bedroom apartment with a roommate. Instead of the Hallmark-card-worthy family gathering with tamales, posole, champurrado, and ponche, I found myself alone at home with an empty refrigerator because my next paycheck was not due to come until New Year's Day. Knowing that tacos at Jack in the Box were ninety-nine cents, I scoured every corner of my apartment for loose change until I found the exact amount I needed, and I immediately burst into tears. *Thank you*, I thought. *Thank you, thank you, thank you. This is all I need. Two tacos, extra hot sauce, and I'll be good.* I pocketed the change, headed to the Jack in the Box down the street, and gleefully placed my order. Yet once the cashier rang me up, I realized I had forgotten to account for tax. My heart dropped to my growling stomach until I heard the cashier say, "Don't worry about it—I got you." Every time I remember this in a moment of financial stress or uncertainty, I am feeding myself a message that incites a calmer feeling and puts me in a place of less resistance. *Even in my biggest moments of scarcity, I am always supported.*

With time and new memories, your new thought patterns will help you to let go of the surviving and coping and rewire your brain with an essential key to the Wealth Warrior mindset: *thriving.*

Bringing down the invisible walls around our financial dreams takes time and effort. It requires the right kind of support, a growth mindset, and our active focus. It's a practice that must be cultivated and adjusted as setbacks arise, but one with incredible returns. Good and bad shit happens, especially when entering the world of investing. As we tackle the next phases of our Wealth Warrior investing journey, our wounds and false beliefs will attempt to ambush us. The keepers of systems in and out of our communities may discourage us from making impactful money moves. Our own minds may betray us by dwelling too much on how we don't have what we want. But now we are armed and ready to face these factors. You are the boss in this relationship.

Pushing these limits, generating our own beliefs, modeling them in our communities—that's how we actualize the opportunity our parents dreamed of for us. That's how we plant our seeds and create our own bountiful garden where we use money as a tool to produce more money to begin building wealth for us, our families, and the future generations to come, so that we all have the freedom to do more of what we desire with our time on this earth. Now that you've survived this emotional boot camp, it's time for the financial one. Let's gooo!

# A SCARCITY MINDSET FINDS AN EXCUSE... A WEALTH WARRIOR FINDS A WAY

Put some respect on my check, or pay me in equity,
watch me reverse out of debt.

*—Beyoncé*

While you continue to look for the clues in your past and your present that will help you understand where your relationship with money stands today and mend the areas that need attention, I want you to take a step in the direction of healing your finances. This journey is not just about being honest and connecting with the emotions that are dredged up by money but also about coming clean with yourself on where you stand in terms of debts (how much you owe) and **assets** (how much you have). This is a habit we need to continue building on to best navigate the stock market investment journey so that we don't allow fear or an overwhelming sense that this is all too much to push us to give up. Don't cop out. I got you. I know how you feel. Seeing the truth about yourself and your relationship with money in black and white, on a page that doesn't allow for justifications or excuses, is fucking overwhelming. It forces us to question our decisions and honestly face our role in taking the right steps to fulfill the future we imagine, whether that be going back to school, buying a home, prepping for retirement, or all three!

As frightening as it may seem, getting clear on your debt will take down the fear factor and allow you to establish the financial goals that are right for you. Hold on—for some of you this may be a bumpy ride, but crawling through the mud will prepare you to march into battle with the confidence every Wealth Warrior needs to triumph.

## GET CLEAR ON YOUR DEBT

Once I started the job at Liberman and settled back into California, I got a call from my cousin Juanita. "So, what are you going to do with all that extra cash now?" That's my girl. She is the first person I considered a best friend in my life. Although we grew up in different states, we had a deep love for each other and were over-the-moon excited when we were able to spend more time together during my family's stints in Texas.

Juanita is one of the most responsible people I know, especially when it comes to money. She has this keen understanding that every drop in the bucket has the power to create something substantial. When I started waking up to my generational wounds, she quickly became part of my money-conscious fam—honestly, she's my hero on that front. I watched her grow and evolve with great admiration and continue to celebrate every one of her accomplishments. By the time she was twenty-three years old, she already owned a house, with a ten-dollar-an-hour salary! With determination and discipline, she managed to save for a down payment through a tanda, a rotating savings and credit association. A tanda is made up of a group of people who know one another and come together so that they can pool their money to save up for a larger goal. Each person contributes a set amount of money, and the sum is then given to one of the members so that they can accomplish that bigger purchase or pay off debt that would've remained out of their reach. This type of association has more than two hundred names and is widely used across Latin America because citizens have a deep distrust of the banking systems in their countries. Immigrants who come to the United States implement this association as a way to access emergency funds or buy a house—case in point, my cousin. The tanda was her money-conscious fam coming up, and it included her parents, who modeled responsible behavior with money.

Juanita's question on the phone that day about my newly pumped-up salary immediately led me to envision a closet full of new clothes, swoon-worthy shoes, and extravagant earrings. While my mind wandered into my fantasy wardrobe, Juanita added, "How about buying a home?" My daydreaming ground to a halt. I was twenty-seven and earning a great salary but still felt unsupported by money. Throughout the years, I had lost trust in it. The "I'm not good with money" belief was in full effect. Yet I was also waking up to the fact that I could no longer hope and pray that it would magically appear in my lap. My first action was accepting the job at Liberman. The second one was finally listening to my cousin.

Juanita was working at a credit union, and that exposure put her at the top of her financial literacy game. She knew the ins and outs of home loans, savings accounts, credit scores—things that I didn't even consider, because my relationship with money was still at a stalemate. "If I can buy a home with my money, think about what you can do with what you're making now," she fervently said to me during that conversation. "All we have to do to get you started is check your credit." I had great respect for her, so I definitely perked up my ears at her advice, but the word *credit* made my stomach do somersaults.

It took months of conversations with my cousin before I finally agreed to request my credit report and face the facts I had been too consumed to pay attention to during the last few years. Who knew such a seemingly small move could have the power to jolt my money wounds awake. I was suddenly flooded with fear, guilt, shame, feelings of failure. Receiving my credit report and sharing it with my cousin almost felt as if I were being asked to walk on fire, naked, in front of a crowd, because I knew it would reveal what I didn't want anyone to see: the unpaid debt hovering over my head like a dagger. Although the trepidation compressed my heart, I took one of the deepest breaths of my life and sent my cousin the report that revealed my financial truth: my racked-up debt and outstanding payments had turned me into a credit card delinquent.

It all started with the first card I applied for, on my college campus, with a 29 percent **interest** rate. I was one of many who fell for the credit card representative canvassing us as freshmen and selling us on the wonders of having cards at our disposal. But just underneath their upbeat attitudes and visions of state-of-the-art dorm furniture was common predatory behavior that many credit card companies employ. What better client than a college freshman with little to no knowledge of how a credit card truly works? Many of us ended up with debt we couldn't afford and opted to not pay our bills and to default. Still, after getting a taste of plastic, I also applied for the Victoria's Secret—you really can never have too much underwear!—and Target cards. I saw those lines of credit like free money. Around a year later, I was in over my head with a $5,000 debt I couldn't pay on my waitress salary. If any of those cards had offered me a larger limit, I'm sure I would've maxed them out too.

So I decided to look the other way and ignore the red-alert past-due statements and collection agency calls altogether. *I'll deal with it later*, I thought. I figured I could pay off the debt once I graduated and started making better money. But "later" went from a few weeks to a few months to five years. In that time frame, I had actually landed jobs with decent salaries, so it wasn't like I couldn't afford to start paying off those bills. But I chose to buy shoes instead. And admitting this was incredibly embarrassing. Juanita had tried to help me get my shit together before. She and her parents helped me identify that I had a serious issue with shopping and that I was likely using it to fill other voids in my life. But change comes only when we are ready to take action.

Facing our debt, our credit score, those numbers staring back at us point-blank from the page, is like airing our dirty laundry. It can feel like we've failed or even wasted our time. But it's also an enormous reality check. A credit score—a number that basically tells lenders your likelihood of repaying your debt—can range from 300 to 850. If you have a higher score, that tells lenders and credit card companies that you will likely make good on your payments. The lower the number, the less credible you become in their eyes. A good score usually falls between 670 and 739. Now, consider this: in 2021, white communities held an average score of 727, while Latine communities averaged 667, Black communities were at 627, and Native American communities held a 612 average. All but the white communities fell below what is considered a good score. This just goes to show that the credit score is an arbitrary number that doesn't paint the whole picture, but there's no room to fill in the blanks, so we need to buck up and get a grip on it.

When we finally come to terms with whatever debt we may be carrying, we are also forced to analyze our spending habits. Where is our money going? What can we do to become more efficient in managing money as a tool rather than letting it become a weapon that can hurt us? Tackling our credit score can become a catalyst to facing our money wounds. Why do we need more

shoes or clothes? What void are we trying to fill? Are these purchases helping or simply covering up something we don't want
to face? Sure, I got caught up in the college credit card scheme,
but I also had a detrimental spending habit that I had to nip in
the bud while taking care of my outstanding debt for this all to
work. While Juanita assessed my financial standing, I walked
into my closet and looked at my collection of mostly cheap shit—
because at the time I preferred quantity over quality—and was
in disbelief with myself. Why had I wasted so much time and
energy on this? The curtain had been pulled, and I didn't waste
a second longer. I Marie Kondo-ed my way through my closet
and apartment before Marie Kondo-ing was a thing. I kept only
what I loved and gave everything else away.

Meanwhile, on the financial front, Juanita sent me a list of
what needed my attention. First up was tackling the debt I could
pay off in full, while making a commitment to myself to diligently pay my current bills so as not to repeat my past mistakes.
My rebellious streak crept up for a minute, and I wanted to push
back on what felt like an impossible task. I just couldn't shake the
shame I felt for having been so irresponsible. But she was stern
and strict with me and helped me stay the course. Now it's my
turn to help you.

Do you know how much debt you're carrying or what your
credit score is? If not, it's time to prepare for battle and get clear
on your debt. Go to www.inluzwetrust.com/wealthwarrior and
download the free Assets and Liabilities worksheet. Grab your
latest bank, retirement, and investment statements and take
the time to read through them and digest the information. Write the

figures that represent how much you have in each account down in the Assets column (what puts money in your wallet). Now take a look at your latest credit card, car payment, loan, and/or mortgage statements and write down what you owe in the Liabilities column (what takes money out of your wallet). Be as detailed as possible. This sheet will simply give you an in-your-face picture of what your finances are looking like today and let you know where you stand in terms of your equity (your assets minus your liabilities). It will also help you start thinking about what kind of money intentions you'd like to set for your future. Revisit this sheet every six to twelve months, and update the numbers to check in with yourself and your progress.

Once you have a clearer picture of where you stand in terms of what you have and what you owe, go online to one of the three major credit-reporting agencies—Equifax, Experian, or TransUnion—to access your credit report. You are entitled to a free credit report every twelve months from each of these agencies, so there are no excuses for not taking this step. The information is available to you; it's up to you to charge onto this battlefield. It's not an easy fight, but it's an enormous reality check that can push you toward a healthier relationship with money, one that can lead to finally building the wealth you deserve.

Once I began to pay off my debt, my cousin drilled into me that I couldn't let this happen again. I couldn't allow myself to fall back into old habits and end up in another suffocating hole of debt and irresponsibility. I heard her loud and clear, but I didn't trust myself to do right. All I could hear in my mind was *I'm not good with money*, that false belief that just wouldn't go away. I knew I needed time to get a better grasp of my finances and cement my new habits. I had to leave behind the little girl who wanted to buy all the sparkly things she hadn't had access to growing up and become a woman capable of managing her money and paying her bills. I accepted that that little girl was not good with money, but that didn't have to reflect the woman I was becoming. Furthermore, if I had the ability to learn new skills, then I could learn how to handle my money too. I just had to put in the work. So I decided to avoid the temptation of a new line of credit to live a life without credit altogether until I put a stop to my bad spending habits and felt I had my shit together.

With time, I went from mindlessly buying stuff to taking a beat and asking myself, *Do I have the money to buy this or not?* If I did have the money, then I'd follow up with *Why do I want to buy this item? Do I need it?* I didn't become restrictive—I still bought things that made me happy, like nice skincare products. Rather, I simply began to gain more clarity on my purchases and where they stemmed from on an emotional front. I realized that buying excessive amounts of stuff just for the sake of it might have made me smile temporarily, but it wasn't bringing me real, deep-seated joy. So I learned to stop going beyond my means.

To become a wealth generator, you need to turn into a warrior who does some major recon on where you stand with your debt and credit. There's no magical way around facing your finances. You must get down and dirty and learn these figures like the back of your hand so you can hold yourself accountable. This is part of the healing journey. Getting clear on your liabilities and assets will help you understand how money is working in your life right now and what you need to adjust to make it work even better.

## GAIN CLARITY ON YOUR MONEY

*Scarcity Mindset:* How much does it cost?

*Wealth Warrior Mindset:* How much does it make?

*Scarcity Mindset:* What if I fail?

*Wealth Warrior Mindset:* What happens when I succeed?

With my financial metamorphosis underway, I jumped at the chance to enter the Hollywood film industry and left my position at Liberman for an unpaid internship at After Dark Films that eventually led to a marketing coordinator job at Pantelion Films, which meant forgoing my $80,000-a-year salary for a thirteen-dollar-an-hour wage along the way. I know, sounds like a huge step back money-wise, but I was convinced it was what I had to do to get my foot in the door. I might not have been able to buy expensive things or treat myself to lavish experiences yet, but I had arrived at a groundbreaking Latine Hollywood film studio that was backed by movie industry giant Lionsgate, and I just felt grateful to be there.

The environment had more of a startup vibe, with the male CEO, CFO, and producer backed up by an all-women marketing team—two executives and two coordinators. Unlike bigger studios, where employees stuck to their specific departments, we were so boots on the ground I tried my hand at every aspect of the business—from budgeting and developing marketing campaigns to coordinating events and coming up with swag bag ideas. Shortly after I joined Pantelion, we landed a major motion picture (*Casa de mi padre*, now considered a cult classic, featuring Gael García Bernal, Diego Luna, and Will Ferrell, who speaks only Spanish throughout the entire movie), and it was our job to produce a red-carpet movie premiere. We needed a stellar PR coordinator to book everything and manage budgets as well as travel, and my two bosses immediately turned to me. "Your personality is so well suited for this type of job, so that's what you'll be doing from now on," they said. I was ready to do anything for this trailblazing studio, so I nodded along, no questions asked. I had been praying for this moment. While having to execute all the logistics with hotels, flights, cars, and press tours and manage $3 million budgets catapulted me into a stress-induced frenzy, the work paid off on an emotional level. I knew I had earned this title, and I was out to prove my bosses right. Within months, I was flying to New York, Chicago, and Miami with A-list stars, working real red carpets at Grauman's Chinese Theatre, living the dream. I was so grateful to have my foot in the Hollywood door, I didn't even think about negotiating a raise. I was a big-time PR coordinator by day and a thirty-one-year-old eating beans and tortillas for dinner and splitting a bottle of Trader Joe's wine with my two roommates by night.

Even though I had taken on an extra boatload of responsibilities and was kicking ass at my job, my salary remained steadfast at thirteen dollars an hour. I deserved a raise, but how could I ask the studio for more money when they were just starting out too? Never once did it occur to me that they were backed by one

of the biggest movie studios on the block. I was totally project-
ing my scarcity and pobrecita yo mentality onto a corporation
with investors! This is a common thought pattern among women
and among children of immigrants. How many times have you
taken on the identity of a company with a valiant mission? Or
treated coworkers like family and ended up doing way too many
favors that upset your workload? Our hardworking, eternally
grateful, humble immigrant or minoritized status urges us to
protect our employers in order to protect ourselves and prove
our worth. This is a massive way that a scarcity mindset, coupled
with oppressive systems and bias, can keep us stunted and struggling. As the daughter of immigrant baby boomers, I figured I
too just had to keep my head down and work hard—false belief
alert!—just to receive a gift on each milestone anniversary until I
could retire and move to Florida with a great pension. The latter
was what I saw modeled on TV, so I powered forward, placing
mutual loyalty above adequate pay.

About a year into my PR role, I was on a plane with none
other than actor Will Ferrell and his publicist, flying to a promotional event in Miami. The publicist walked over from first
class to my coach seat and mentioned something that needed to
be purchased before our upcoming stop. I nodded along, going
into PR mode, fully ignoring my racing heart. "I can't solve this.
I need to call my boss." He gave me a WTF look and just walked
away. As soon as he was out of sight, I quickly texted my boss.
"Just put it on your card and we'll pay you back," she replied
matter-of-factly. Logging in furiously, I glanced at my checking
account balance...I barely had enough to make rent, which was

due in a week. What's more, a couple of weeks prior to this incident, I had reached out to HR to request a tax block when my car broke down. They didn't withhold any taxes from that cycle's check, so I had access to a few extra bucks to cover the repair. I had no money to spare.

Usually, all costs were covered with the CEO's personal credit card and later reimbursed to him, so this totally came out of left field for me. There was no way I could afford to let go of my hard-earned cash and risk not making rent. "Hello?" My boss's puzzled text snapped me back to the present. Feeling the heat of embarrassment flush my cheeks, I replied, "I don't have a credit card." Ever since I faced my credit report and put my financial cleanup to work a couple of years earlier, I had vowed to not get in debt again, so I'd quit credit cards completely. Just the thought of using my debit card made my heart rate peel rubber, with my scarcity mindset at the wheel.

My boss took the helm and reached out to the PR team we contracted on the ground in Miami, and the issue was resolved, but I was no less mortified. Once our event wrapped and I was on my way back home, my initial shame soon turned into anger. How could I be putting in so much time and energy at a company that was paying me thirteen dollars an hour *and* expecting me to cover expenses on my own dime? This feeling stuck with me.

Given my role in the studio and all the responsibilities I juggled (with grace and enormous patience), I decided to take matters into my own hands and go straight to the CEO to plead my case. "I need at least one more dollar per hour," I said at our scheduled meeting. I figured if I kept my request for a raise low enough, I'd have a better chance at getting his okay.

"Unfortunately, our budget is so tight, we can't offer any type of raise at this time," said the CEO, without giving it a second thought.

I left his office downcast, feeling the weight of the world on my petite frame, but I also learned a valuable lesson that day. That was the first time the need for a monetary change eclipsed my emotional investment in the studio. These people weren't my family. They were my colleagues, and they were looking out for their business. Now it was my turn to look out for me. With this thought, the CEO's *no* suddenly shook the fighter within me awake and fueled my desire for more.

Gaining clarity on your money is absolutely essential to fully assessing your financial scope before you jump into any wealth-building action, whether it be asking for a raise, changing jobs, or allocating money to invest in the stock market. You don't just need to be clear on your debt; you have to know what you're working with in order to figure out what you need to move forward successfully.

Go back to www.inluzwetrust.com/wealthwarrior and download the free Investment Plan balance sheet. How much do you bring in monthly in salary, interest income, side-gig income? Add those figures to the Income column. How much do you spend monthly on groceries, utilities, cable, subscription services, clothes, entertainment, credit card payments, rent or mortgage payments, and so on? Write those figures down in the Bills and

Subscriptions column. This is your chance to see where your cash is coming from, where it's going, and what may or may not be working in your wealth-building favor. Keep this sheet handy, as we will be revisiting it in Step 4 to fill in the remaining boxes.

As you review these numbers, take a moment to also check in with your emotions. Ask yourself, *How am I feeling right now?* Be honest. Do you trust money? Do you feel supported by money? Are you ready to go or do you need a minute? It's okay to feel doubts or insecurities creeping in. Each step in this journey takes time, patience, and the ability to attentively tune in to not just your actions but how you're feeling and why in the process.

When I faced my credit report, I had given up on myself in that area of my life and was in complete denial. But as soon as I stared this fear in the face and understood what I needed to focus on so that I could receive and expand my wealth, pieces of my life finally began to shift for the better. I was able to automate financial processes, thus freeing up some of my mental space and time (which systems and keepers often rob from us) and, in turn, giving me the clarity to see that I was being overworked and underpaid. When you face your liabilities and gain clarity on your money, there's a sense of accountability and responsibility that fosters invaluable growth and understanding and gives you the room to heal and attract opportunities that will serve you better in all areas of your life. And it readies you to confidently begin to harness some key money moves that will usher you into your wealth-building journey in stride.

## TAP IN: TOP SIX WEALTH-GENERATING INVESTMENTS

Like any impending battle, entering new territory can cause fear and anxiety (what's up, money wounds?!). Maybe you're terrible at math or you didn't have parents modeling a positive relationship with money. Maybe you're starting out like I did a decade ago—with no real generational wealth, several people to take care of, and an awareness that the road to wealth is long and uncertain. I'm here to tell you that *now* is the time to get financially lit—literate, that is. So before we do a deep dive into the stock market, let's get your feet wet and start building your confidence by learning about the top six wealth-generating investments that are either readily accessible or within most people's reach.

These moves multiply your dollars while you earn your primary income. They will also build your credit and a **financial portfolio** (a.k.a. your collection of investments), which can later be used as leverage for more wealth-building strategies. Remember that financial ease will flow from your newly reframed beliefs. With time, you'll be able to rest assured that your money is growing while you take on the world, and when you're ready to buy that new car or cash out on a vacation, your financial portfolio will support it. If you already have some of these components in place, great! If you don't, it's always a good time to start leveraging them in your favor. I highly recommend jumping in sooner rather than later, as these are all investments that will gain value over the months and years. It's time to start deploying your money to work for you.

## 1. Pay Yourself First with a High-Yield Savings Account

"High-yield savings accounts are for poor people." When I heard that sentence, it really fucking shook me. I was sitting cross-legged on my couch with my laptop, deep in my financial literacy journey, checking out YouTube videos and every other free resource I could find online to better understand money. I had come upon this young white guy who seemed to have a fresh take on explaining finance, and I was all in on listening to his advice until he said that sentence. Wait a minute... if a high-yield savings account is for poor people, where does that leave everyone in our communities who put away their hard-earned cash in a regular savings account that was marketed specifically to them?

My initial reaction was to shut him down, but instinctively my heart said, "Don't reject it." So I reeled in my desire to furiously type up a comment to give this guy a piece of my mind and instead sat with his statement, attempting to get what he was trying to say rather than whom he was talking about. And then it hit me. We take great pride in hoarding money, without realizing that wealth and riches are made out of investing. But in order to shift our mindset and get to the point where we can become comfortable with investing, we need to start making certain tweaks in what we do with our money today. And it can start with something as simple as moving your money from a regular savings account to a **high-yield savings account**. When I asked my friends and family if they knew about high-yield savings accounts, all I got in return were blank stares. Honestly, I had been clueless about this once too. Hell, I didn't even use my savings account until the summer of 2012, when I left Pantelion and landed a content specialist position at Netflix, which put me back in the higher-wage group, making $75,000 a year.

Having already done my financial audit and put into practice better money habits, I was fully aware that I had to take this major pay bump seriously. I wasn't about to blow it all on shoes or clothes anymore. I started off with a short and doable list of priorities, which included fixing my car and moving in with my partner, Alfonso. For the first time, I wasn't letting my emotions preside over my decisions. Instead, I budgeted both expenditures to make sure these priorities wouldn't put me in the red, and then moved forward with them.

As I diligently and consciously figured out my next steps in this newfound financial realm that was suddenly accessible to me, I befriended a dope German immigrant, Nadine, who soon became my work bestie at Netflix. She had more experience in film operations than I did, so she turned into somewhat of a guide, helping me navigate this new workplace, making sense of the endless list of acronyms and explaining the company's preferred processes. She also openly discussed her finances with me, and how she had set up automatic transfers to build up her savings account. My wealth-conscious ears perked up.

"This month, my goal is to save one thousand dollars," she said one day. Seeing a bolt of interest light up my face, she added, "Let's do it together!"

I replied with an immediate and resounding, "Yes!"

I was intrigued by this woman who had no problem talking money with anyone she met. It wasn't a stigma in her culture. She was actually pretty shocked that in the land of milk and honey, we didn't openly talk about the milk and honey.

"Okay, so how much do you want to have in your savings?" she asked me, urging me to set my very first long-term financial goal.

"Ten thousand dollars," I said shyly, feeling that was a lofty objective for me. I had never seen even a thousand dollars in my account in my lifetime, so envisioning ten grand felt somewhat like an audacious and insurmountable peak.

Noticing my reaction, she added, "You have to envision the amount like it's no big deal."

It was a big deal for me, but I understood her advice. I had to make it feel less overwhelming, almost as if we were going on a healthy-eating kick together. To make it feel like a conquerable goal, we divided the ten thousand up into smaller monthly targets that felt more practical and mentally accessible. I also recalled a piece of crucial advice my cousin Juanita had delivered before my financial audit: "Always look for banks that will pay you the highest interest rates."

Money loses its value every year because of **inflation**. Prices of goods go up, so it takes more money to buy those tortillas and papas for your tacos de papa. Therefore, the dollar becomes less valuable over time. Interest rates help us keep our money's value in check, so *where* we store our money matters. Different banks and accounts offer different **APYs (annual percentage yields)**, which are the real rate of return earned on an investment. In other words, the return on the money you deposit in a given year. A good APY helps you preserve some of your money's value that's lost from inflation. Now, keep this in mind: when we diligently put money in our savings accounts, our dollars and cents are not just sitting in boxes somewhere in the bank with our names written on the sides—the bank spends it. Yeah, you read right. Banks lend our savings to another customer in the form of a mortgage or loan. Moreover, the banks lend that money out at a higher interest rate or invest our money in the stock market to make a higher return for themselves. In other words, they make money off our money because they need to do whatever it takes to maintain the currency's value. It's the hidden cost of the service of storing our money. With a measly national average APY of 0.07 percent on regular savings accounts at the time this book was written, you are far from being compensated properly for their use of your money.

A high-yield savings account is the first move you can make to start shifting this imbalance in your favor, if ever so slightly. Let's say you have $5,000 in a regular savings account, which pays an APY of 0.10 percent. You would earn a return of $5 over the course of one year. Now, if that same $5,000 were in a high-yield savings account that paid 2 percent interest, you'd end the year with an extra $100 in your account. We're talking a $95 difference in your favor! Some high-yield savings accounts offer APYs up to twenty times that of regular savings accounts. These accounts are usually only online, so by not having to pay for rent or utilities or tellers, they are able to pass these savings on to you in the form of a higher interest rate. But if you're not ready to hand your cash over to the internet, some banks that offer high-yield savings accounts do have brick-and-mortar stores now.

## WEALTH WARRIOR TACTICS:
### *SIMPLE INTEREST VERSUS COMPOUND INTEREST*

Let's say you deposit $5,000 into a simple interest high-yield savings account with an interest rate of 2 percent. **Simple interest** is the money you earn on the initial **principal** amount borrowed or deposited—in this case, that $5,000. So you end up with $5,100 at the end of the year, and the next year you'll make another $100 off that initial $5,000, and so on just like my cousin showed me. This type of interest typically pertains to money borrowed for a mortgage or car loan, and deposits into bank accounts.

Here's where it gets interesting. **Compound interest** is the amount you earn on both the principal amount you deposit *and* the accrued interest. Let's say you deposit your $5,000 and you accrue $100 in interest after a year. With compound interest, both amounts will accrue interest at a 2 percent rate the following year. This continues to compound year after year. With compound interest, you'd make $5,520.20 in ten years on your initial investment versus just $1,000 with simple interest. Compound interest accounts typically pertain to IRAs and savings accounts. This is the type of account you are looking for.

Like anything of importance, choosing the right account will require research on your behalf. This is your chance to start strengthening your financial literacy muscle through research and taking action that fits your needs. Not all high-yield savings accounts are created equal; some have trade-offs, like fees for benefits like higher APYs or waiving ATM fees. Once you settle on an account, they're a cinch to open. You can get started with a Google search for banks that offer high-yield savings accounts or take it a step further and search for Black- or Latine-run banks, by typing key words such as "POC-owned banks" or "Latine-owned banks." When you reach a bank's website, use this list of common offerings and stipulations to assess if it matches up with your needs:

✓ **FDIC insured:** The Federal Deposit Insurance Corporation, or the **FDIC**, is an independent federal agency that safeguards your deposits in the event your bank fails because of an economic downturn. The standard maximum insurable amount for an FDIC-insured account is $250,000. This means that if anything happens to the bank, up to $250,000 of your money will be protected. Making sure your account is FDIC insured is your biggest safety net and is highly recommended when signing up for an account.

✓ **APY:** We've got this one down, but to review, the annual percentage yield on an account, or the APY, is the return on the money you deposit in a given year. You can narrow your list of accounts down by choosing the reputable, FDIC-insured banks offering the highest APYs. APYs are constantly changing, so make sure to find each bank's most up-to-date information and check back regularly once you've chosen an account.

✓ **Fees:** Always read the fine print! Some accounts may have overdraft or other hidden fees, and getting hit with a hundred-dollar fee right before payday is *not* a part of our Wealth Warrior journey. Do your due diligence—there are plenty of high-yield savings accounts from reputable institutions that will not charge you monthly fees.

✓ **Minimum balance:** Some banks require you to have a minimum balance in your account to avoid fees; others do not. If you can, opt for the latter.

✓ **Deposit requirements:** When opening an account, some banks require a minimum deposit, usually $25 to $100, but others do not. It's important you know what is being asked of you in case this is a deal breaker.

✓ **Transfers and deposits:** Make sure you can link your high-yield savings account to your personal checking account and brokerage account so that you can easily transfer money among your existing accounts.

✓ **ATM card:** High-yield savings accounts usually allow only six transactions and ATM withdrawals per month. Others allow unlimited withdrawals via ATMs or tellers with their debit card. It's good to have the option of having an ATM card if that is something you think would be useful to you, but I don't necessarily advise it. Having an ATM card means you'll have easy access to your savings account, which can make withdrawals that much more tempting. So if you're swipe-happy, step away from the card.

✓ **Intuitive apps and customer service:** This is not a deal breaker, but if you can find an account that also offers an easy-to-use app, it will make your life easier when having to make transfers or mobile deposits, especially if you choose an online-only bank. Note: although you can't go to a physical location for online-only banks, many offer 24/7 customer service via phone or chat, so make sure you look for these options.

If you're not sure how to choose the right account for you, consider using well-known resources like NerdWallet or Investopedia that offer a side-by-side comparison of different accounts. They make it easier to decide whether you're okay with a minimum balance to get a higher APY. Or to determine the best accounts to help you avoid fees, if you know that's where you tend to get tripped up. Whatever your parameters, once you've chosen your preferred high-yield savings account, keep your list of runners-up handy. This way, you can opt in and out of accounts to get the most from your money, especially when you start feeling comfortable and seeing your savings grow.

---

**WEALTH WARRIOR TACTICS:**
*HAVE MORE THAN ONE HIGH-YIELD*
*SAVINGS ACCOUNT*

Since interest rates fluctuate regularly, I maintain two high-yield savings accounts and one credit union account. That seems like a lot, but I empower myself by taking a pulse check on the rates every six months or so and transferring my money to the one paying the highest interest at a given time. This exercise will serve as a foundation when you start dipping into the stock market, because it helps build your confidence around moving money and making tactical choices. Of course, we're just starting with researching and opening one account here, but nothing is more empowering in the financial world than learning how to manage and take ownership of your money.

---

At Netflix, I was making three times as much as I was at my previous job and my overhead remained about the same, so I managed to set aside enough to reach my $10,000 savings mark about a year after I opened my high-yield savings account. I couldn't contain my pride and excitement. It was the most money I had ever had in my life. But that also opened the door to a restrictive side of me I hadn't experienced before. I had worked so hard to get my relationship with money under control that now that I was receiving and accumulating real money, I didn't want to squander it. Suddenly, I became obsessed with keeping my savings account balance at no less than $10,000. I couldn't even stand seeing it at $9,999. Then one day, while catching up with Nadine, she said, "Guess what? I'm going on vacation to an all-inclusive resort in Mexico! It's so beautiful and high end, I can't wait!"

"You are?!" I exclaimed, staring back at her in disbelief. "But what about our savings goals? What do you mean a vacation?" I was so confused. Up until then, even though she had more money than I did, we'd both go shopping at LA's renowned flea market, the Santee Alley. She didn't splurge on expensive brands or big-ticket items. To hear her say that she'd booked a stay at a luxury resort was like experiencing a small earthquake in my financial world. Yet as I wrestled with her decision, my shock turned into a feeling of empowerment. It was like a veil had been lifted—I realized I was in the presence of a full-fledged woman who had her shit together. Her example was giving me permission to relax a bit and allow myself to have a little fun along the journey.

After a long pause, I recapitulated and said, "You know what? I really want to do that too." I just didn't know how. After working so hard to get my finance issues under control and finally beginning to accumulate real money, I just couldn't bring myself to spend any of it. My mind was reeling with thoughts of potentially being only one vacation away from losing it all—not just the money but also my job. Time and again, I ran through these worst-case scenarios where I might need to use my savings for imaginary emergencies, and that drove me from carelessly spending money to carefully hoarding it. Yet this type of thinking can lead to a life of deep-rooted fear and self-deprivation.

"You have to stop being so restrictive, Linda," said my friend, touching my shoulder and looking me straight in the eye after I openly expressed my desire to follow in her footsteps. "You can't save all this money only for emergencies. You deserve to treat yourself with the finer things in life too and reward yourself for reaching your milestones," she added, calmly imparting yet another golden nugget of wisdom.

I spent the next week scouring the internet in search of cheap, all-inclusive hotels and flights within my budget. And I found a crazy deal for $1,400 that included flights. Since my partner, Alfonso, would pay for his half, it came down to only $700 a pop. Note: I'm not advocating for spending your entire savings on a luxury vacation. I crunched the numbers, and that was less than 1 percent of my savings, an amount I knew I could put back in there in the next couple of months tops, so I booked it.

The next day, when I ran into my friend at the office, I blurted out, "I'm going on vacation too!" She smiled wide and was quick to celebrate this moment with me, unknowingly also showing me how wonderful it is when we come together to cheer each other on.

By encouraging me to take a little slice of my savings to reward myself for reaching this milestone, my friend showed me how to pay myself first by allowing myself to have an enriching and relaxing experience, which in turn taught me how to let money go and make space for more to come in. With time, as this experience sank in, it made me realize that the way I viewed my emergency fund needed a serious revamp. Out of every emergency, there's always a chance for growth. What's more, that money we so diligently save up doesn't have to be *solely* for the shit-hit-the-fan moments in our lives. We need to stop catastrophizing about what hasn't happened yet. By flipping this switch and keeping money in this account for not just the bad but also the good, we are saturating it with better energy. *Pay yourself first* means taking the course that will improve your skills, signing up for that summit that could lead to amazing networking opportunities, purchasing that book that will inspire you to charge toward your dreams. Anything that builds your knowledge is an investment in yourself that will likely help you course-correct your scarcity mindset and catapult your personal growth. That's why nowadays, I prefer to call what we have long referred to as our emergency fund an *opportunity* fund. It gives us the opportunity to grow our savings, to save our asses in case of an emergency, and to enjoy life and invest in our wealth-building journey.

## 2. Get Yourself a Certified Public Accountant

Every warrior needs a solid tactical operator who possesses the knowledge and training to carry out intelligence and counter-surveillance to prepare us for any outcome so that we can eventually triumph on the battlefield. In the financial world, this tactical operator is called a **certified public accountant**, or **CPA**, a wealth-generating ally who will help us get our income taxes in order so that we can continue to grow our money successfully. Listen, I'm all for DIY projects, but when it comes to taxes, getting a good CPA should be at the top of your list. After all, income taxes are one of the largest liabilities (together with car loans, mortgages, and credit card debt, to name a few) we incur on a yearly basis. Your CPA is there to assess the current state of your taxes and educate you on tax strategies you may not be aware of. Ultimately a good CPA will not only save you money; they'll also know how to create it based on your current situation.

When I began working at Pantelion, income tax season was like Christmas. My coworkers were buzzing, already making plans for what they would do once they received that year's income tax refund. I, on the other hand, dreaded that April 15 deadline. "I don't know how you do it," I said to a coworker, dumbfounded. "I make so little money, and I still owe taxes at the end of the year." That was how I had been operating since I began filing income taxes—it was normal to me. I figured it was just my luck and that was how the system worked.

My boss overheard our conversation and immediately stepped in. "No, Linda, it sounds like you have a bad accountant."

In the decade or so that I had spent in the workforce and paying income taxes, that had never crossed my mind. I thought all tax consultants followed the same list of rules and formulas and therefore would come up with the same final numbers, until I met my CPA, Andy, a Harvard-educated Mexican-American who chose to provide his high level of experience and service to people of color, along with our immigrant communities.

In our first meeting, Andy explained to me how tax returns work. And then he dropped a truth bomb that I repeat at the start of every tax season: "Be careful not to get too excited about your income tax refund—most people don't realize that most of it is already their money." The government doesn't give us free money; that money has been ours the whole time; it's merely being held as a prepayment. Sometimes we pay more taxes than owed throughout the year—this is a calculation your CPA will reach after they do your income taxes based on a variety of factors such as your tax rate, dependents, and work circumstances—and you get a refund of money you prepaid. I had no idea this was how it worked until Andy explained it to me so that I understood why he was asking such specific questions about my everyday habits. He was searching for money in the form of deductions or credits in every corner of my life. He did a deep dive and looked into every financial move I made, including large and small purchases and even the most meager contributions to my opportunity fund.

Even though Andy was saving me money, my deep-seated feelings of shame and my pobrecita yo mindset threatened to bubble to the surface with every question he posed...and then I got angry. Not at Andy, but at my previous tax consultant. How could he have missed so many opportunities to help me save my hard-earned cash? Up until that point, I had been made to believe that the government was out to get us, that income tax season was a bust for everyone, and that my tax consultant was totally submissive to the powers that be. Andy was far from begrudging; he helped me see that there were laws in place that could help me make (or, in this case, keep) more money. He empowered me by explaining I was exercising my rights as a taxpayer, based on current income tax laws, to claim deductions and credits owed to me. I hired him that afternoon, and we still work together to this day. Juanita gave me the tools I needed to embark on my wealth-building journey, and Andy did the recon so that I could prepare to slay the battles ahead. He began sharing his financial wisdom with me from day one, back when I was at Pantelion, then he guided me through my moneymaking years at Netflix. And he was instrumental in setting up my business. His education and perspective have had and will continue to have a long-lasting impact on my wealth-building journey.

Behind every successful person is likely a great CPA. Ask your friends for recommendations; identify the people you know who have money and manage it well, and ask them for recommendations. When interviewing a CPA, remember that just because they have a certification and experience doesn't mean they can't have money wounds too. In retrospect, I can clearly see my previous tax consultant had straight-up fear in claiming certain expenses that I now know pertained to my job when I was working on commission only. That type of job entitles us to a plethora of credits, deductions, and expenses, but I remember my tax consultant not wanting to claim them. This is a red flag. If you have the type of job that requires out-of-pocket expenses, ask your potential CPA up front how they would handle that for you or what they would recommend. If you ask for advice and they give you nothing in return, you may want to interview someone else. If there's a lack of questions pertaining to what you do for a living, no suggestions on how to better handle your current and future financial goals, or no guidance taking into account your current yearly income, that is another red flag. Another good question to ask is if they have other clients in your occupation or profession. That's always a plus because it means they probably know a slew of tax strategies that could benefit you. You don't want someone who is hands off and only a preparer; you want a partner and collaborator, someone who's got your back.

Take it from me—this will be one of the most important investments you make. If you need a little more convincing, here are some of the leading benefits of having a CPA on your side while on your wealth-building journey:

- ✓ **Up-to-date guidance on changing tax laws:** Are you keeping up with your state and federal tax laws? If you're DIYing your taxes on an online site or with your trusty TI-84, there's a high chance you may not know that the laws change on a yearly basis. And if you're thinking, *Linda, I do my homework*, consider that you might be spending some of your precious time learning tax laws that might not even pertain to your industry. Part of a CPA's job is to stay up to date on tax law changes so they can do their very best to turn the specifics of your profession and enterprises—whether it be art, business, or a trade— into tax savings.

- ✓ **Tailored tax strategies:** Let's say you're cutting costs by handling your own taxes. This is the reality for many, but ultimately, the amount that you save by not hiring a CPA is incomparable to the amount you save from tapping into your CPA's crucial tax-saving strategies that pertain to you as an individual. They will be able to help you navigate those big life moments, like if you have a child or come into an inheritance, as seamlessly as possible. And their experience allows them to easily draw from similar cases with other clients and use those assessments in your favor.

✓ **Tactical advice on how to set up your business:** When I first expanded my spirituality podcast—which I began in 2016 to document my personal journey of self-healing in hopes of empowering others to do the same—into an event production business, I wasn't bringing in much income. Like any new endeavor, it would take time, dedication, and Wealth Warrior know-how to truly blossom. At that point, I needed resources for my small business. My CPA recommended that I start with a DBA (doing business as), which allowed me to do business under a different name than my own, and as the business has grown, we've reassessed our tactics to scale up my setups so I can meet my needs, protect myself, and save as much as I can on taxes. If you have multiple income sources or a business venture that needs to be set up or is in the process of scaling or growing, a CPA will be your right-hand person. We need you, as family and community members, to model what is possible when we have a good CPA preserving and protecting our income so we can go on to multiply it.

✓ **Estate planning:** As if all the aforementioned benefits weren't enough, CPAs can also help you make a plan for your money after you pass away. As hard as it may be to think about this, it is also a key component to building generational wealth. My CPA has been mentoring me on setting up the best plan for my children once I am no longer here, such as creating a living trust.

Remember: your time is money. Research shows that self-filing taxpayers spend an average of 8.8 hours filing their taxes. That's a full business day during which you're actually losing money because you're spending your time on your taxes rather than on your work or business. While hiring a CPA may cost money up front, you will also be saving time in the long run, not to mention receiving invaluable knowledge along the way, so lean into that. No matter what, find someone who has your best interests in mind and is on your team, so you too can start saving money and use it to build more wealth.

## 3. Open a Roth IRA

A Wealth Warrior can't keep fighting endlessly. There will come a time when we will need to hang up our weapons and simply tend to the bountiful garden we have fought so hard to create. That's why it's important to start thinking about our future today.

In 2019, when my business began to generate a solid income, my CPA suggested that I consider investing in a **Roth IRA**. (Note: if you have a 401(k) through your employer, you can also invest in a Roth IRA if you meet the requirements. You may also contribute to a Roth 401(k) if your employer has a qualified retirement account. They are not mutually exclusive, so keep on reading.) I had heard about individual retirement accounts before, and I understood that these were accounts I could open on my own in addition to any employee benefits I was receiving, but I hadn't paid much attention to them, because I was holding on to my money so tightly I couldn't fathom putting any away for the distant future. But when my CPA assessed my lack of retirement savings, he told me that opening a Roth IRA wouldn't just be a way to help me reach a comfortable retirement, it would be beneficial for me now in the form of possible tax breaks. If only I had known this sooner! *Please note: I'm sharing this knowledge with you to open your mind to the investment possibilities within your reach through this specific type of account. As always, do your own due diligence. If you want to learn more about the Roth or any other type of retirement account, talk with your CPA.*

A Roth IRA is an individual retirement account that allows you to contribute after-tax income and let it grow tax-free. The APY will depend on your contributions as well as the investment options, such as mutual funds, stocks, bonds, and so forth, so make sure to talk to your CPA to learn more about this account and figure out where you want to invest this money. After we turn fifty-nine and a half, we are allowed to withdraw our money tax- and penalty-free, so long as the account has been open for at least five years. If you don't need to dip into your Roth at fifty-nine and a half, you can continue to keep it open until you're ready to withdraw funds. Furthermore, if you pass away, your children and/or beneficiaries will receive your Roth IRA as a tax-free inheritance. In other words, they will be able to withdraw this money tax-free too.

Here's the catch: you can open a Roth IRA only if you make less than a certain amount a year—currently, the yearly income limit is $144,000 if you file your taxes as a single person and $214,000 if you're married and file jointly (*check with your CPA, as the income limit is subject to change on an annual basis and differs based on your current filing status*). If you're under the age of fifty and your income falls below the limit that pertains to you, then you are allowed to contribute a maximum of $6,500 before the next income tax filing deadline, and $7,500 if you're older than fifty (again, check with your CPA, as these numbers are subject to change).

As mentioned previously, investing in a Roth IRA will not lower your taxable income, which is the money you receive in exchange for your work—the income tax benefit will come at the time you withdraw this money. This was one of the biggest reasons why I began investing in my Roth IRA in 2019. I am not only saving and preserving my money for the future but also putting my money to work for me. Again, please check with your CPA; this will not be everyone's case, but it is a possibility.

Because I didn't have a retirement account to begin with, Andy suggested I open a **traditional IRA** along with my Roth IRA. A traditional IRA has the same contribution limits as a Roth IRA; however, a traditional IRA does help you reduce your taxable income and, hence, your income tax owed is reduced by your pre-tax contributions. That's why the traditional IRA is considered a tax-deferred retirement account. In other words, your money grows untaxed and income taxes are paid at the income tax rate you have at the time of withdrawal only when the money is distributed or withdrawn. If you are fifty-nine and a half or older, your distribution and/or withdrawal will not be subject to penalties. However, if you are younger than fifty-nine and a half, your distribution and/or withdrawal will be subject to early withdrawal penalties. Unlike the Roth IRA, where you can store and grow your money for as long as you'd like, with a traditional IRA there is a required minimum distribution beginning at age seventy-three.

Last but not least, both Roth and traditional IRAs earn compound interest (the amount you earn on both the principal amount you deposit in your Roth *and* the accrued interest). Any interest you earn in these two accounts does not count as income unless you make an early withdrawal; therefore, it is not taxed. Having said that, although other investment accounts may have different tax implications, that should never stop us from investing. Fearing income taxes is directly linked to our scarcity mindset; it prevents the expansion we deserve. Remember: the intention throughout our wealth-building journey is to preserve our capital and build on it.

---

### WEALTH WARRIOR TACTICS:
### *THE BACKDOOR ROTH IRA*

If your income exceeds the Roth IRA income limit threshold, you might want to ask your CPA if the timing is right for you to convert your pre-tax traditional IRA to a Roth IRA (check with your CPA, as the income limit thresholds will change, along with your income tax strategies). The backdoor Roth IRA strategy is a legal tax strategy to get around the income limit thresholds that usually prevent high-income earners from contributing to Roth IRAs. Note that you will pay income taxes on any funds that have not been taxed previously. The upside is everything you gain after that within your new Roth IRA is tax-free, with all the benefits mentioned previously. This strategy is best if you have a sabbatical-type year or a calendar year with significantly less income because it's an exceptional way to reduce your future income tax **liability**. As always, first and foremost, check with your CPA before making any of these financial moves.

## 4. Invest in a Health Savings Account

Another wealth-generating investment you might want to consider is a **health savings account (HSA)**, which acts like a regular savings account as well as an investment account. Its intended use is for qualified medical deductibles, copayments, coinsurance, and qualified long-term-care insurance premiums and services, as well as other medical expenses, which include approved items—such as cough and cold medicines, baby-care essentials, or some skincare products with SPF—you can buy at your local pharmacy or at online HSA stores.

To qualify for an HSA, you must be enrolled in a high-deductible health plan. Like with the traditional IRA, pre-tax contributions may lower your income taxes because you may deduct your HSA contributions from your federal income tax.

Earnings in this account grow tax-free and distributions used to pay for qualified medical expenses are also tax-free.

Unlike contributions to a flexible spending account (FSA), which you have to use within a year or lose it, unspent money in your HSA rolls over to the next year.

Withdrawals for nonmedical expenses are allowed before age sixty-five but are subject to a penalty plus income tax. Withdrawals for nonmedical expenses after age sixty-five are subject only to your current income tax rate. Like both the traditional and Roth IRAs, this account also has a yearly contribution limit, which, right now, for an individual, is $3,850, and $7,750 for a married couple filing jointly (*again, check with your CPA, as these limits will fluctuate*).

It gives me peace of mind to know that if I do have a massive medical emergency that my health insurance does not cover completely, I can tap into my HSA to pay for that medical expense. Like IRAs, there are tax implications pertaining to these types of accounts, as well as laws that are constantly changing, so I highly recommend you seek professional help before making any of these moves to make sure they are the best fit for you and your financial needs.

**WEALTH WARRIOR TACTICS:**
***ADD BENEFICIARIES TO CREATE***
***GENERATIONAL WEALTH***

All the accounts I've mentioned so far (high-yield savings accounts, IRAs, and HSAs) allow you to add a **beneficiary**, a person or entity who will receive these accounts once you pass away. By setting up your beneficiaries, you're planting the seeds for the next generation's financial health after you are gone. Check with your financial institutions and your CPA to learn more about the beneficiary rules for each type of account. It will save your family from huge financial headaches and ensure that your assets go to the intended beneficiaries.

## 5. Real Estate: It's Complicated but Worth It

Real estate is the investment that gets the most hype in our communities. Most people dream of owning their own home; that's why parents, relatives, society, seemingly everyone wants us to start investing in real estate as soon as we can. My mom bought our condo in her late twenties, and as soon as I hit adulthood, she started breathing down my neck about home ownership.

By the time I was edging toward my fortieth birthday, with no home to my name, I felt like my mom saw me as a straight-up failure. If she was able to buy a place as an immigrant who spoke broken English and cleaned houses, then what the hell was my problem? Many of us are raised hearing that once we purchase our home, we have it made, because the possibility of owning a home is part of the American Dream most of our immigrant ancestors were promised when they came to this country. The truth is that the path to owning real estate is different for everyone. For some, like my cousin Juanita, it might happen sooner in their lives. For others, like me, it might happen later. Some people may not even be considering it yet, because they feel they don't have the means to reach this goal. But it is possible and there are different ways of obtaining the required down payment to embark on this wealth-building investment. Many use their savings accounts (by now I hope yours are all high yield!) to diligently save up for this purchase. Depending on where you live and the price of real estate in your area, this might take more or less time, of course. Others, like me, do it their own way. Instead of focusing on building up my opportunity fund for this particular goal, I invested in the stock market and used some of the money I made in gains (money that the market generated for me beyond my initial investment) over the course of seven years to put a $120,000 down payment on my first home, in Dallas, Texas.

Maybe you're still saving up for this big purchase. Maybe I'm preaching to the choir because you're already a homeowner. But did you know that while your home can be a powerful investment when it comes to generational wealth, it is also one of the biggest liabilities you can obtain, oftentimes propelling you into a system of debt? The bigger the mortgage, the bigger the liability. I'm not here to talk you out of purchasing real estate— it is hands down one of the most common wealth-building investments—but it's important to understand what it means to your finances.

That said, history has proven that it is never a bad time to buy a house. Some may read this and think, *Wait, but what about the housing market crash in 2008?* What created that crash were terrible predatory subprime home loans that increased with time and were given by bank institutions to people who shouldn't have been approved for those loans to begin with. Signing on the dotted line for these types of loans was our decision, and we need to take responsibility for our part in this mistake. That's the thing about investing: it is our responsibility to do our due diligence and understand what we're getting ourselves into before diving in. So why is it never a bad time to buy a house? Because, like having a baby, there's usually never really a right time either.

There will always be something we have to compromise on with this type of investment, either a high interest rate or a roaring housing market. But historically, although the value of a home may fluctuate in the short term, a property always **appreciates** (increases in value) with time. Currently, the average long-term return on investment in real estate is 8.6 percent. That's what makes it a powerful way to build wealth. Once you pay off your mortgage, that home will be considered an asset. You can also get tax breaks for property **depreciation**—that is, when your property decreases in value—and a low mortgage rate can help you leverage funds that you can use for another investment, such as stocks or a new property. Furthermore, your home has a level of value because it has **equity**—you can figure this out by subtracting all loans on your home from its market value (that is, the value it would have if it were for sale in that moment). Plus, no one can manufacture more land, so when we buy land, we're automatically purchasing something that will also appreciate over time.

Now, if you want to turn a piece of real estate into an even bigger wealth-building asset, it needs to generate money for you beyond its yearly increase in value. In other words, a home is cash-flow positive when someone else (a tenant) is paying you money to rent it. If that rental income covers your mortgage, taxes, and any other fees, *and* leaves you with a profit, congratulations, you've got yourself a kick-ass wealth-building asset. What's more, we can't leave the landlord role to white men alone. We need better landlords who care for our communities; that's why we need more communities of color participating not just as first-time home buyers but as real estate investors.

I'm a proud homeowner, but knowing this is a liability and not an asset in my overall portfolio at this time, I have my eyes set on purchasing an investment property—a place I can turn into an income-producing venture, a powerful stream of income that would allow me to give some of my relatives work so that money can begin to flow into the rest of my family. This is where generational wealth thrives, because it opens the doors to not just ownership but to jobs that can be shared with our families and communities. Anytime I find a property that I think may meet my requirements, I take it to my CPA to analyze the neighborhood and crunch the numbers.

Becoming a homeowner is satisfying. Becoming an investment property owner is money-multiplying. Both are valid goals, so long as you understand how they each play out in your overall portfolio of assets. Knowledge is the ultimate achievement.

## 6. The Real MVP: The Stock Market

I have high-yield savings accounts, a fantastic CPA, a traditional and Roth IRA, and an HSA. I'm also a homeowner, and I'm working on purchasing my first investment property. But if you were to ask me what wealth-generating investment is my most valuable player, I'd say, hands down, the stock market. It's the only way you can obtain and build an asset immediately, versus the long process of saving money or purchasing a property. There are no minimums needed to get started, no credit check or work history required, no boxes to tick or hoops to jump through. All you need to open a brokerage account and participate in this exponential potential for income growth is a social security number or an individual taxpayer identification number (ITIN). A **brokerage account** is an investment account that gives you access to the stock market so that you can buy and sell stocks as well as other investments. Some banks offer brokerage accounts, but there are also companies that focus solely on these types of accounts. You will need a brokerage account to start your wealth-building investment journey. There is a clear explanation of how to open your brokerage account in Step 4; for now, I just want you to become familiar with this term and its meaning.

When you open a brokerage account, you can purchase stock as soon as your initial deposit has cleared (which usually takes a few business days) and automatically have an asset in your possession. You won't need a down payment, you won't have to go through a complicated application process in which you sign your life away, and the application can't be turned down because of the color of your skin or your last name. No one can stop you from buying stocks if you have a social security number or an ITIN and a few bucks to spare. A high-yield savings account or your IRA may make your money work for you and set you on your way toward long-term goals, but they won't make you real money, the kind that can be life changing and help you build significant generational wealth. They're the safer steps you can take to begin shifting your money mindset. But that's just the kickoff to change your perspective on wealth; it's your training ground. Now we're about to enter the battlefield that will eventually lead you to the bountiful financial garden you and your family deserve. The time has come to suit up, rally your courage, and take up a space that is rightfully yours to claim. You are ready to take the next step. Prepare to receive an arsenal of knowledge, Wealth Warriors: your stock market journey begins now.

# STEP 3

## CONQUER THE LANGUAGE OF THE STOCK MARKET

A dollar might turn into a million and we all rich.

—*Kendrick Lamar*

A successful Wealth Warrior should always become familiar with the lay of the land before entering a battlefield. Now that you're aware of your money wounds and you've warmed up your wealth-building muscles with foundational investment strategies, you're ready to take your boot camp to the next level. It's time to dive in and figure out what the stock market is. I'll share with you some basic shoptalk and break down the common terms, definitions, and categories that are key parts of your investment journey.

Take your time with this new language. If you feel your money wounds begin to activate, maybe you start to feel a little overwhelmed or tight in the chest, revisit earlier chapters to set

your compass toward the reframed beliefs of our Wealth Warrior Truths. Soon you'll start to feel empowered to take up space
in this powerful territory. Until then, you can check out the
glossary on page 251 to look up definitions when in need of a
refresher. You got this.

## THE STOCK MARKET...
## LET'S BREAK IT DOWN

When I was a kid, I used to go to the swap meet in Santa Fe
Springs, California, with my parents every weekend. My uncle
and aunt had a stand where my parents and I would help sell cas-
settes. I loved this vibrant scene filled with business owners from
all backgrounds and corners of the world making sales amid
the chaos of clamoring voices and bustling energy. The big blue
tents sheltered us from the piping-hot sun. I felt extra important
standing on my aunt and uncle's side of the table, like I belonged
to the team. The early-morning hours were for laying the cassette
tapes out on the table. We always had Juan Gabriel, Los Tigres del
Norte, or some other music playing in the background to inspire
the passersby to stop and check out the tunes that could be theirs
for a small price. Sometimes, if my uncle and dad were busy, I'd
point the customer in the direction of what they were searching
for or jump in to help them find it fast before they lost interest.
Timing was everything. As the day progressed, my eyes would
wander to the other sections of the meet where vendors sold toys
and clothes. But we were not there to shop; we were there to help

my uncle and aunt sell. This was when I started to understand the exchange of cash for something in return.

The **stock market** is basically like a swap meet, el tianguis, or better yet, a grocery store. It holds different stocks, which are pieces of publicly traded companies, much like a grocery store holds different products from different brands. Any one of us can own a piece of a **publicly traded company**, because, as the name suggests, it is a public company.

In order for a private company to go public and come to the market, it must fill out application forms to explain what it does, where it's heading, how much money it has made, and its potential for growth. This information is then scrutinized by the **Securities and Exchange Commission (SEC)**, an independent agency of the US government that regulates the stock market and protects investors. If the SEC approves the company's application, then it is allowed to go public and join the market. This means that we the public have an opportunity to own a piece of that company, because it is now a publicly traded company. We are currently already investing in countless companies by purchasing their products. The stock market gives us the opportunity to purchase a piece of the companies that produce our favorite products, so that we can capitalize on any growth that these companies may experience through **capital gains** (the profit made from an initial investment).

These publicly traded companies in the stock market are organized by sectors. There are eleven different trading sectors, known as **market sectors**. In each sector, you can find publicly traded companies that provide similar goods and services. These sectors are like the different aisles at your grocery store. When you walk through the grocery store, you have a dairy aisle, a meat aisle, a frozen foods aisle. Stores are set up this way so we can be efficient when shopping there. We know exactly where to go to easily access what we need. That's the way the stock market is set up too. The eleven sectors of the stock market include consumer staples, communication services, consumer discretionary, energy, financials, healthcare, industrials, information technology, materials, real estate, and utilities. The market is divided into sectors to help keep it organized and measure its performance against peer companies, but we don't necessarily pick our stocks based on sectors. We usually first pick a company we're interested in and later identify what sector it belongs to. For example, when you go to the grocery store, you have a list of groceries that you want to purchase. Those are your stocks. You're not buying groceries based on what aisle they're in. You're buying groceries based on the products you want to get. Once you grab the products from the aisles (we will get into stock-picking specifics in Step 5), you head over to the cash register to conduct the transaction. That cash register is equivalent to a stock exchange in the stock market.

**Stock exchanges** are the infrastructure and formal mechanism where shares are listed and exchange transactions are made, facilitating the trading of stocks (a.k.a. equity securities). There are two leading stock exchanges in the United States: the National Association of Securities Dealers Automated Quotations (Nasdaq), where the buying and selling of stock happens solely online; and the well-known New York Stock Exchange (NYSE), which connects buyers to the stock market through either electronic trading or physical floor trading. Think Wall Street, which is an actual street in Downtown Manhattan and has long been synonymous with the financial industry.

When I was seventeen years old and cruising through my junior year of public high school in Dallas, I applied and was accepted to DECA, which per its mission statement is a program aimed at preparing "emerging leaders and entrepreneurs in marketing, finance, hospitality and management in high schools and colleges around the globe." This program didn't just give me an amazing overview of the marketing and business skills needed to excel in the real world; it also offered eye-opening field trips. Our trip senior year was to none other than New York City. Our teacher had scheduled a full itinerary with several sites she wanted us to visit while we were there, including the Statue of Liberty, the Empire State Building, Times Square, and other tourist attractions. One day, we had two activities scheduled at the same time; half of the group went to see a live taping of *The Sally Jessy Raphael Show*, and the other half went to visit the NYSE on Wall Street and ring the famed bell that signals the opening and closing of the market each day. I was super bummed when I got placed in this second group, because I really wanted to go to the show. Although I wasn't really into the talk show host, I loved the idea of participating in a live taping.

Yet when we arrived on Wall Street, the sight of that colossal building with imposing columns towering overhead immediately erased any leftover desire I had to be a part of the other group. We climbed up a few steps, and inside we came upon the main trading floor of the stock exchange, fifteen thousand square feet filled with screens and professional traders bustling around the narrow pathways, anxiously waiting to start the trading day. A man in a crisp suit led us up a staircase to the podium overlooking the entire trading floor.

---

### WEALTH WARRIOR TACTICS:
#### *STICK TO TRADITIONAL MARKET HOURS*

Just like your local grocery store, stock exchanges operate during specified hours, called **market hours**. Traditional market hours are Monday to Friday, 9:30 a.m. ET to 4:00 p.m. ET. There are also **pre-market hours** (Monday to Friday from 4:00 a.m. ET to 9:30 a.m. ET) and **after-market hours** (Monday to Friday from 4:00 p.m. ET to 8:00 p.m. ET) for big institutions that move massive amounts of money. The industry calls them whales, or institutions moving other people's money, and sharks are shrewd and aggressive independent investors. We are the tiny fish. Any time whales move money in the stock market—sometimes millions or billions of dollars—the price of a stock can swing relatively quickly, making it a volatile moment to buy or sell. As a new investor, I recommend you stick to traditional market hours. I have over ten years of experience in the stock market, and I still prefer to do my investing within traditional market hours.

I glanced across the NYSE, taking it all in yet not fully grasping the moment, and was overcome by the dynamic energy in the air. A few of my classmates rang the ten-second bell signaling the opening of the market, and the crowd below cheered loudly and then swerved around and instantly started yelling into their phones and thrusting pieces of paper they no longer needed in the air. I could sense that something incredibly significant was happening in this space. Although it was all new to me, I was aware that I was in a room with decision makers whose choices would affect the global economy, and that energy had a massive impact on me. It was exhilarating, a seed of something bigger to come in my life.

The stock market gives us access to more by providing us with the opportunity to become what is termed a retail investor. A **retail investor** (a.k.a. an individual investor) is a non-professional investor who buys and sells stock. Whether you're a beginning investor or a more seasoned one with ten-plus years of experience like me, you can take your wealth into your own hands and go straight to the market yourself to purchase stock.

## STOCKS AND SHARES: TIME TO KNOW WHAT'S WHAT

So, we've arrived at the grocery store—I mean, the stock market—with the intention of buying a piece of a publicly traded company during traditional market hours. But what exactly are those pieces? They're stocks. A **stock** is divided into shares; these shares make up a publicly traded company. Let's take it back to the grocery store. We're inside, and we head over to the fresh produce aisle (our chosen sector) because we're interested in buying apples. We reach the bins and see that there are several beautiful towers of apples in stock. In other words, the companies have stock, and you are there to purchase shares (individual apples) of that stock. **Shares** represent the fractional ownership of the publicly traded company you're investing in. If you buy one, two, or three apples, they become your share of that stock, making you a shareholder of the company that produces the apples. But wait—there are different categories to consider when buying stocks.

## CATEGORIES OF STOCKS

Think of the categories of stocks as different brands of similar products. Some are older trusted brands (blue chip stocks), others are seasonal brands (cyclical stocks), and still others are cheap generic brands (penny stocks). Knowing what category your stock falls in will allow you to identify that one investment is more or less risky than another. That's why it's important to understand the companies you're investing in. Note that some stocks can fall into multiple categories, and some categories may feel similar to one another. There are nuances that distinguish them, so as we move on to the next chapters and begin to discuss how to pick your own stocks, we'll revisit these categories for guidance. For now, let's get down to understanding what they each mean.

✓ **Blue chip stocks** are well-known, high-quality companies that are leaders in their industries and have stood the test of time. They're like social media accounts that have been blue-check verified. These include Apple, Coca-Cola, Johnson & Johnson, Disney—the OG companies. Blue chip stocks are a safer investment that will likely provide growth year after year, as long as they continue to create products we're dependent on.

✓ **Cyclical stocks** are seasonal stocks that we cycle through. They include airlines, retail companies, hotels, and restaurants. The value of these stocks depends on a season—like summer or the holidays for travel companies—and the economy, as they can take big hits when there's a major national or international event. During the height of the COVID-19 pandemic in 2020, Marriott, Cheesecake Factory, and Delta stocks dropped dramatically and lost their value. We've also seen them in steady recovery since then, as travel and dining out have picked back up. I don't own any cyclical stocks—I can feel bigger investors rolling their eyes now and thinking, *Ugh, she doesn't even own cyclicals.* They like them because the stock value will usually go up seasonally, but I find that irrelevant. I prefer stocks that are gaining no matter the season. Each journey is different, so we'll learn together how to choose the best option for you.

✓ **Defensive stocks** are well-established companies, like those in the blue chip category, but they provide consistent dividends and stable earnings regardless of the state of the overall stock market. Some examples are Costco and Coca-Cola. Yes, defensive stocks sound similar to blue chip stocks, because they are. Stocks can fall into more than one category, so Coca-Cola, for example, is considered a blue chip, defensive, and dividend stock. As consistent as this category of stocks is, the pandemic pushed them to their limit and took them down for a short period of time. So we've now seen that if the overall stock market hits a huge crisis, these stocks will be affected too, if only temporarily.

✓ **Dividend stocks** reward you with a **dividend** (a payment made separately on your investments) when they generate profits. When you buy a dividend stock, not only do you get to see gains from the growth of the stock, but the company will pay out a percentage of its quarterly or annual profits (depending on the company). Some examples of dividend stocks include Target, Clorox, and Walgreens. In 2022, Target paid out $0.90 quarterly, and Clorox's quarterly dividend was $1.16. So if you owned five Target shares, you would have received $0.90 per share, which would've equaled a total of $4.50 in dividends. The most I've ever seen is $6.00, but that amount is far from the norm. Note that when you receive dividends, you do have to pay income tax on that money. You must also own the stock for a certain period of time before you are rewarded a dividend.

✓ **Growth stocks** offer a growth rate that is substantially higher than the overall market average of other stocks. They typically do not pay dividends, because they are growers, meaning their value will increase with time. These stocks are great for people looking to play the long game, because growth usually happens in the long term, but don't be fooled by their name—even though they're "growth" stocks, like all stocks, there are no 100 percent guarantees that they will grow. Some examples of growth stocks include Amazon, Google, and Tesla.

✓ **Meme stocks** are stocks that have gone viral on social media platforms and chat communities. This virality causes a wave of people to buy them at once, jacking up the stock price with overnight growth of about 30 percent to 50 percent. It's not normal for stocks to rise like this overnight. And it by no means signifies the company is worth more—that is why these stocks are so dangerous. In many cases, these are organized efforts by trading communities, almost like a Wall Street betting ring, with bettors hoping to strike it rich. A good example is what went down with Game-Stop. That was basically an antiestablishment play. A Reddit user shared why he thought GameStop was undervalued, and he showed how much he had invested. He started with $25,000 and then bought another $25,000. People started feeling **FOMO**, so they started buying in. In early January 2021, the stock was at $2.57 a share, and by January 28 it was at $483.00. Some media outlets picked up this story, and it became a wildfire spreading all over the news, inspiring more investors to jump in. That guy who started it all ended up making $48 million with his $50,000 initial investment. When retail investors see the value of a stock skyrocket overnight, it's difficult for them not to start to feel FOMO, but that emotion drives them to start buying in when a stock is at its peak. However, like the latest dance craze or celebrity scandal, viral moments don't last. That's what makes these stocks dangerous—they're not conducive to growth for long-term investors. In fact, you may overhear you invested in a **stonk**, which is an intentional misspelling of the word *stock* used ironically to underline the losses typically incurred by meme stocks. Even professional traders need precise knowledge to get in and out at the right time. Becoming a Wealth Warrior doesn't include get-rich-quick tactics because we're in it for the long haul.

✓ **Penny stocks** are stocks of a small company that are typically traded for less than five dollars per share. The price can be tempting to investors with a tight budget, but note that penny stocks are extremely speculative—in other words, they're an enormous gamble, turning the stock market into a casino. I don't recommend that new investors buy them.

✓ **Speculative stocks** are stocks at the beginning of their growth stage and are therefore extremely high risk. You're betting your money and hoping that this stock will produce a product that will succeed at disrupting the industry and manage to sustain that success in the future. But we don't know for sure if it's going to make it or if it's going to tank, which can create an opportunity for high gains or losses. Many of the companies that are now categorized as blue chip stocks were once considered speculative, so I do like to buy a modest amount of speculative stock.

✓ **Tech stocks** are any stocks involved in the technology sector, from semiconductor producers to software providers. I like these stocks because they disrupt the way we're living, accommodating the new world we're entering. They allow us to watch brand-new movie releases without having to leave our homes, order a product online and have it delivered in less than two days, request a taxi through an app, charge our electric cars in our garages, have a computer in our smartphones, and so forth. Some examples of tech stocks are Apple, Tesla, and Amazon.

✓ **Value stocks** are those that have been around for a long time and have grown into industry leaders with little room to expand, but are seen by many as reliable business models. Some experts believe they are being sold for less than what they believe their value to be, while others think that they're value traps and cheap for a reason. Some people specifically search for value stocks, while others avoid them like the plague—it's all relative and will depend on whom you ask. Some examples of value stocks are Bank of America, Toyota, and Verizon.

I suggest that when choosing categories of stock as a new investor, you start with blue chip stocks, which are one of the safer ways to begin to get exposure in the market. Steer clear of any speculative or penny stocks, which are incredibly volatile and unreliable. Just to put this in perspective, I started investing in speculative stocks only after *eight years* in the stock market, and they still represent only 1 percent of my portfolio, because I understand that although I may believe in a company, its potential does not guarantee its future. The last thing I want you to do is gamble away your hard-earned cash as you begin your investment journey. Solid investments will give you a much better chance at long-term returns.

---

**WEALTH WARRIOR TACTICS:**
*KEEP A WATCH ON CRYPTO*

With the dawn of blockchain technology and cryptocurrency, our generation is watching the birth of a new digital currency or asset class. Wall Street is waking up to it. El Salvador has made it legal tender. The goal of cryptocurrency is in the name: *currency*. It's openly tracked on a blockchain, which provides a virtual accounting system that is open for the public to review.

Contrary to traditional currency, which is managed by a centralized authority (like the Federal Reserve System in the United States), the cryptocurrency system is decentralized, which makes it attractive to many yet also risky because it is not regulated. When a currency or asset class is not regulated, anyone can make fake coins without anyone else catching on, because there is no entity tasked with verifying whether coins are legit. Furthermore, when cryptocurrency's value began to skyrocket, it made more sense to keep it than to spend it. This, in turn, made crypto start trading like a stock, fluctuating with the market instead of being another form of currency with which we can purchase goods and services. Because of this, when the stock market tanked in 2022, so did the value of cryptocurrency, making it incredibly volatile. I do think it's an important asset class, but it's too early to tell its true value and potential.

If you're considering cryptocurrency as an investment, start by doing your research on the top-performing coins that have so far stood the test of time. Also make sure that you own your crypto wallet, a place where you can securely keep your coins, and have your own private key. If you don't own a wallet or the keys to your wallet, you might be invested in crypto without actually owning it. I do believe block-chain technology is the future, but I'm also keeping a watchful eye on it to see how it evolves. If this is some-thing that interests you, please do your due diligence, dig deeper to become familiar enough with it, and see if you're comfortable participating or not.

## FRACTIONAL SHARES AND STOCK SPLITS

Something new that has happened in the last few years in the stock market is what the industry calls **fractional shares**—in other words, fractions of a full share of a company. Let's say you're at the bin filled with green apples and you want to buy one, but you find out that each individual apple costs a whop-ping hundred dollars, which is way beyond your budget. Now you have the option to buy a slice of an apple. That slice is a fractional share. The amount of money you pay for the slice, or fraction, will be proportionate to the size of the slice. So if you have twenty dollars, your slice will be smaller. If you have fifty dollars, your slice will be larger. Once you make this purchase, you become a fractional share owner. With time, you will be able to return to the store and buy more slices until you are able to own one whole apple, or share. It's a budget-friendly way to access and participate in the stock market.

Here's another scenario: the green apples are in stock, but there are a lot of people walking into the store wanting to buy one of them. This sudden demand, in turn, jacks up the price of each apple. There aren't enough in the bin to go around, so only specific customers with bigger budgets can and will purchase apples at this price. So the apple company decides to produce more apples. By doing so, they lower the cost of each share, and there are more to go around. This company decision to increase the number of shares is called a **stock split**. When the amount of apples in stock increases based on how many apples (shares) already exist, the cost of each individual apple will go down. This means more people will walk to this stand and actually be able to purchase these apples because they will now be within their budget. Now investors on a budget can purchase a share of a stock that they might not have had access to before. Yes, they could've bought fractional shares, but oftentimes people take a lot of pride in the amount of shares they can obtain—splits are great for these types of investors.

Wait a minute—so what does a stock split mean for shares you already own? Let's say you bought one green apple yesterday, and the company decided to do a four-to-one stock split today. That means that for every apple, or share, that exists, including the one you own, the company has decided to give you three more. In other words, you go from owning one apple to owning four. This also means that for those apples that are not owned by anyone, there will now be three more available to purchase in the bin. In a stock split, each apple is now worth a fraction of the original apple's price. So if your original apple was valued at a hundred dollars, each apple is now worth twenty-five dollars. You still have that same hundred dollars' worth of stock, but divided into four shares. Note, although very rare, **reverse stock splits** can also happen, especially if a company's share price falls too low and it may be at risk of being delisted from the market.

Contrary to a stock split, a reverse stock split of, say, one-for-four would mean that your four apples would become one, so you would go from owning four shares to owning one share of that stock. Therefore, if each apple was at a hundred dollars, and you had four apples with a total value of four hundred dollars, with a reverse stock split, you would now have one apple worth four hundred dollars.

Stock splits got a lot of hype in 2020 when Tesla and Apple did this with their stock, and then again in 2022 as companies such as Google and Amazon took on the same strategy. Companies do stock splits as a strategic way to get more people to invest in them. Those who couldn't invest now have the opportunity to do so, and those who were already invested now own more shares, each of which have potential for growth. When people buy up more and more shares, the value of the stock usually goes up. Interestingly, many old-school Wall Streeters actually hate stock splits. Even though nothing is changing about the business, making stocks more accessible to people crushes investors' bragging rights about owning shares that are worth, say, $3,000 a pop. But at the end of the day, they can't keep us out of the game! We are living in the system these keepers created, and the only way we will eventually be able to change the game is if we learn how to play.

I want you to get deeply acquainted with this fundamental knowledge so you are armed with the tools you need to successfully step into the Wealth Warrior arena of investing. I'm so proud of you for getting this far! After such an arduous battle, give your mind the necessary time to process what you've learned so far. Allow yourself the space to clearly envision the stock market as a grocery store, notice the correlations, metabolize this new language, and start incorporating it into your daily life. Once you feel comfortable enough to take your arsenal to the battlefield, turn the page to learn how to open your brokerage account.

## STEP 4

# SLAM THE DOOR ON BROKE AND OPEN YOUR BROKERAGE ACCOUNT

Ellos me abrieron la puerta, yo la partí más abierta.
Aquí los límites se quiebran, nosotros vamos con fuerza.
Yo vine a cobrar.*

—*Snow Tha Product*

We're about to enter the arena where the savviest people across professions congregate to build wealth. Now more than ever, you need to join this front line, so that in five, ten, fifteen years you are meeting and exceeding your financial goals, have a strong portfolio, and are accessing the wealth-generating space that

---

* They opened the door for me, I kicked it down even more. Here we break limits, we come with force. I came to collect.

has always been rightfully yours. Doing so will allow us to help reduce the financial disparity we experience today and make a significant change for generations to come. As you navigate this entire process, you will begin to experience firsthand how money can work as a tool in our wealth-building journey—that's one of the reasons I see the stock market as our ultimate teacher. Our investments today have the potential to turn into a dream vacation, a down payment on a home, a college fund for our kids down the line, and more. Wealth Warriors, take a deep breath— we're charging into this new field of operations as a united front.

## REMEMBER: SCARED MONEY
## DON'T MAKE MONEY

Two months into my job at Netflix, I walked into an office ablaze with chatter and kinetic energy. I didn't know what the hell was going on, but it probably had to do with it being the morning after the company's third-quarter earnings call. As usual, I just beelined it for my desk, which was sealed off by tall tan cubicle partitions, and busied myself with the start of the workday. A white higher-up who was cool with my colleagues and me zeroed in on my cluelessness, so he quietly walked over and said, "Hey, Linda, did you listen to the earnings call?"

"No. As long as I get my paycheck, I'm good," I replied, try- ing to shut that conversation down. Sure, the call was about the company's earnings, but I didn't think it concerned me. All I wanted to do was focus on becoming a dream team player so I could keep my newly minted salary and reach the long-term savings goal I had recently set with Nadine.

Likely sensing my apprehension, he just nodded and walked away. A short while later, I caught sight of his clean-shaven face framed by short dirty-blond hair in the small mirror hanging above my monitor. He was standing at my cube's entrance and seemed eager to talk, so I pulled out the small cushion-top metal filing cabinet and invited him to take a seat.

"Have you started investing in Netflix?" he asked me.

My heartbeat felt like it had crawled into my throat, the pulse resounding in my hot ears. He was asking me about something completely out of my depth, and I would have to figure out a way to nonchalantly doggy-paddle to shore.

"Stocks shot up after yesterday's call, and we all made a killing. You need to get in on this, Linda."

Impostor syndrome was using my confidence as a punching bag in that office, but so far, I had managed to nod my way through conversations that went over my head. I understood the gist of what he was trying to tell me, but he saw through my fake knowing look, so he didn't push any further, changing the subject while I secretly breathed a huge sigh of relief.

The next day, this coworker, who for some reason was unwilling to give up on me, popped into my cubicle again, this time with his cell phone in hand. He started talking to me about the stock market and investing, doing his best to use layman's terms to hold my attention rather than talk down to me. My insecurity and shame about not knowing how to speak this new language made me feel annoyed that he'd come back to pester me, but a part of me quietly craved to step into this foreign world of wealth. As I sensed his genuine interest in opening my eyes and getting me on board with this opportunity, I began to feel more at ease in the conversation and even dared ask "What does that mean?" when he mentioned a word or phrase I didn't recognize. Then he unlocked his phone and showed me his investment portfolio. "Look, this is how much I made after this quarter's earnings call."

I stared at those unfamiliar tables and graphs in silence.

"Linda, you already have insight on this business. You know where it's headed. You need to use this insight in your favor and play the game."

During the following weeks, he made a habit of swinging by on break to continue showing me the market's ebb and flow and how Netflix's stock was performing. He urged me to focus on where the business was headed and what it could possibly accomplish, helping me see the company from a completely new perspective, that of an investor rather than an employee. Each time he left my cube, I'd wheel over to my computer and quickly Google the terms I didn't quite grasp, whetting my financial literacy appetite. I spent the rest of 2012 hearing my colleague out while also reading up on anything and everything I could get my hands on regarding the stock market, familiarizing myself with the company's financial statements, listening to previous earnings calls, and checking out the stock charts, hoping the barrage of information would stifle my fear of entering this space.

I'd always been told that you needed thousands to get started in the market. I was also scared it might turn out to be the get-rich-quick scam everyone in my community always said it was. And it's not like we were completely wrong to believe this. Some people do in fact use the market as a gambling tool, speculating what stock will go up and down and trading on the fly to make some extra cash overnight. With that as the prevailing image in my experience, I thought, *Why stir the pot just when all the ingredients in my life have started to comfortably simmer?* To be honest, I hadn't even dared put money into my 401(k), which my employer would've matched—that's free money right there!— so you can imagine the level of anxiety I felt when considering the stock market. To top it off, I had no one in my life modeling investment behavior other than this colleague, and he was white, which played into my belief that the market was really only for white people. But I decided to bite the bullet and listen to my thunderous gut, urging me to take this leap.

## SET MONEY INTENTIONS

Before I began to invest in Netflix stock, I looked out into the future, at what this money could eventually do for me, and I saw a house. I set that intention and committed to not selling out of my shares for at least ten years, unless my goal was met sooner than that. The end result I envisioned with this money was to move the capital gains out of the stock market and turn it into equity, which I eventually managed to do when I purchased my first home. I wholeheartedly believe in keeping our actions in alignment with our intentions in every area of our lives, including financially. Before we head into stock-picking territory, stop and ask yourself, *What are my money intentions?* The answer can be anything from purchasing a home or building a college fund for your kid to making $100,000. Your money intention will be your driving force and motivation as you begin this new chapter in your life, especially when you hit a snag for the first time. When in doubt, focus on your money intention and remind yourself why you decided to enter this wealth-building arena to begin with.

My intention for you is that you gather the tools provided in these pages and use them to begin taking part in the stock market as a long-term investor so that you minimize your risk and learn how to build wealth over time. Opening your brokerage account is a revolutionary act that will give you access to the free market, which has long seemed out of reach to communities of color. Taking this important step will not only allow you to level up your money moxie but also empower you to become a bona fide Wealth Warrior. We're just getting started!

## ESTABLISH YOUR BUDGET: ONLY INVEST
## WHAT YOU CAN AFFORD TO LOSE

I thought long and hard before establishing my initial investment budget. Since I was still pretty skeptical of the stock market, I decided to simply focus on a figure that wouldn't plunge me into a state of total panic if I lost it all. An easy way to find this magic comfort number is to put it in perspective with your own life. If you tend to regularly spend thirty dollars on a nice T-shirt you don't really need, then maybe that's the number that's good for you. If you're used to spending a hundred dollars at a restaurant with your family without giving it a second thought, then maybe that could be your monthly target. Go back to your Investment Plan worksheet and tally up the numbers in the monthly summary box to see how much you have left over. This will give you a clearer picture of what you might be able to afford to lose from that sum. Come up with a few options, and pay attention to your body's response. Which one tenses you up? Which one makes you feel relaxed? Choose the latter.

I ran my numbers, revisited my balance sheet to measure my income against my debt, and took into account the money I had already begun to deploy into an opportunity fund. I could afford to lose about $2,500 a year—$208 a month, to be exact—so that was the magic comfort figure I used to solely purchase Netflix stock. Let me be clear: I didn't *want* to lose that money. Deciding this amount up front meant that I could give myself a full year to experience the stock market. If by the end of that first year I did not feel comfortable or satisfied with how much I made in the market, I would sell my shares and call it a day. Or if things took a turn for the worse, an unexpected event would not disrupt the rest of my financial portfolio. In the case that things went better than I expected, I'd stay the course on my ten-year plan. This freedom to choose gave me peace of mind from money wounds and my scarcity mindset.

When you set out to establish your own budget and choose what you can afford to lose, I want you to remember this: the money that you choose to let go of is actually money you are using to pay yourself. In other words, when you receive your income, you will basically be sending a few dollars out to go and replicate in the market for you. The idea of deploying money into the market and letting it work for me was completely new in my world. I still use this "only invest what you can afford to lose" strategy to prevent fear from stopping me cold in the middle of my wealth-building path.

The beauty of the stock market is that you can start with as little as $20 a month, or even $10 if that's all you can afford to invest right now. If you choose to deploy $100, $200, or $1,000 a month, that's great too. Ultimately, it's not about the amount so much as building consistency in setting this money aside for your stock market journey.

Once you've come up with a number you are comfortable investing, hold on to that first month's deposit so that you have a stash ready to take action when you reach that milestone. The most important investment you can make is in yourself. Are you ready?

## OPEN YOUR BROKERAGE ACCOUNT

Once I determined that I could afford to spend $208 a month in the market, I signed up for Netflix's **employee stock options**. While filling out the form that our HR department provided, I checked off the box that said Netflix would automatically deduct the $208 from my paycheck. The company then opened a brokerage account for me and handed me my log-in and password. Piece of cake, right? For those of you working for a larger company with a strong presence in the stock market, sure. But for the vast majority, opening a brokerage account is a frightening and confusing process. As the years passed, I committed myself and my business to breaking this barrier and helping others in my community take this necessary step. I'm on your side too. Knowledge is power, so let's start by understanding the account you're about to open.

A brokerage account is an investment account that gives you access to the stock market. You can use your brokerage account to invest in stocks, bonds, and IRAs—in other words, all types of financial assets that can be bought, sold, or gifted. All you need to open your brokerage account is a social security number or an ITIN, and a completed registration form. That's it. There's no credit check, no work history requested, no charge to open the account, and no minimum amount to get started. What's more, if you're a DACA recipient, you too are eligible to open this account and invest in the market.

As people of color, we often have to turn over our long list of sufferings just to gain access to schools, jobs, loans, and other opportunities. But as you can see, this is not the case when it comes to opening a brokerage account. You don't have to regurgitate your entire life story in hopes of being approved here. All you have to do is get down and dirty with your research skills and choose the right brokerage firm for you.

A **brokerage firm** brings buyers and sellers together to expedite their transactions in the stock market. Going back to our grocery store analogy, choosing a firm is like choosing what supermarket you want to shop at. You need to find the one that will provide the goods and services that satisfy your financial needs. Some of you may like to hit up your local Ralphs, while others may prefer Walmart or Trader Joe's. I know I sound like a broken record, but all I ask is that you do your due diligence and choose a reputable and widely recognized brokerage firm to open your account.

To get you started, here are four of the most recognized, long-standing firms in the United States, all of which are accessible online:

- ✓ *E\*Trade.* Founded in the early eighties, it officially became the pioneer of online brokerage firms when it launched its digital platform in 1992.
- ✓ *Fidelity Investments.* A well-established and highly regarded company, it has been around since 1946.
- ✓ *TD Ameritrade.* Another one of the major online brokerage firms in the country, it was established in 1975 and was recently acquired by Charles Schwab.
- ✓ *Charles Schwab.* Founded in the early seventies and considered "America's largest discount broker," it continues to be one of the leading brokerage firms in the country.

Some of these companies may sound familiar—you may have an IRA or a 401(k) with one of them through your employer. If so, consider continuing this leg of your investment journey with this company, because you not only already have an individual brokerage account there but also have established a financial relationship with this firm and can leverage both of these factors in your favor when opening an additional account. As I mentioned, I didn't choose my brokerage firm, but once I entered the market, began to navigate this online platform, and did my own research, I decided it was a solid and intuitive choice for me, so I've stuck with this firm ever since.

If you don't have an account yet, then narrow this list down further by researching which company meets your needs the best. For example, E*Trade doesn't offer direct purchase of fractional shares, so if that's something you're interested in, you should look into firms like Fidelity or Charles Schwab, which do. Furthermore, if you think you will be investing on the go, then you want to make sure to choose a company that offers an intuitive app that you find easy to understand and navigate. And no, I'm not talking about an automatic investment app; that would defy the purpose of this book. I don't want AI to pick stocks for you; I want you to learn how to pick your own stocks. According to the Federal Reserve, in 2019, only 15 percent of Americans held direct stock. Let's change that by joining this group and expanding that percentage to include not just more Americans but more communities of color.

Each brokerage firm has slightly different forms that you need to fill out to open your account. All of them will ask what type of brokerage account you want to open—an individual account for yourself; a joint account, which you'd share with a partner; or, in some cases, a custodial account for your child (they must be under the age of eighteen). They'll also ask for your personal information, like your name, address, phone number, email, birthday, government-issued ID, and social security number or ITIN; and your employment details, such as your occupation, your work location, and contact info for your employer if you're not self-employed. From there, you'll have to make some decisions about the account itself. Let's break it down.

*Options, margin, or future trading.* When asked if you want to add one of these choices to your account, just say no for now. These choices are aimed at far more experienced investors, and they require much higher levels of trading skills. If later in your journey you want to dive into these specific niches, then you can always go back and add them to your account, but make sure you know what you're getting yourself into first. For example, an account on margin means you're basically investing with money borrowed from the broker that will accrue interest. Because the money is borrowed, brokerage firms then have the right to force you out of holding those assets if the stock drops enough—that's called a margin call. Margins are a really dangerous way of investing because you are held accountable for that money. Highly experienced investors are able to navigate this rocky road, but thankfully, you don't need to take on such risk to be a full-fledged Wealth Warrior. If you later decide you want to know more about what these choices mean, contact your CPA or a trusted and experienced member of your money-conscious fam before you add the option to your account. (Note: if the choice comes up, pick the cash balance program, which allows you to earn interest and is insured by the SIPC, a.k.a. Securities

Investment Protection Corporation, which, like the FDIC, safe-guards up to $250,000 of your deposits.)

*Investment objectives and risk tolerance.* Many firms will ask you to list your "purpose," "expected use," or "goals" for your brokerage account. Some common goals in your firm's drop-down menu may include the following:

- ✓ Active/day trading
- ✓ Investing for college / a minor
- ✓ Investing for estate planning
- ✓ Investing for retirement
- ✓ Investing for tax planning
- ✓ Learning how to invest
- ✓ Long-term investing with occasional transfers

I find this list mind blowing because it gives insight into the level of access you can gain when you open a brokerage account. From investing in the stock market for your children's college tuition, for your retirement, or to get ahead of tax season, to simply learning how to invest, these options are available to our communities. And it is high time we start using them to our advantage too. According to Gallup, 56 percent of Americans own stock. The wealthiest 10 percent of Americans own 89 percent of that stock. And get this: of the percentage of stocks owned by Americans, 90 percent are owned by white people while only 1.1 percent are owned by Black people and 0.4 percent belong to Latine people. We have the power to change this by entering the market now. Since we're just getting started on this Wealth Warrior journey, I suggest you choose the "learning how to invest" goal. The first couple of years of investing will be all about learning through doing. My role is simply to introduce you to the market and help you see it as an accessible space for you. The market will be your teacher, money will be your tool, and with time, your wounds and emotions will no longer dominate your wealth-building decisions.

Another common drop-down menu will offer the following options to define your objectives:

- ✓ Speculation
- ✓ Growth
- ✓ Income
- ✓ Capital preservation

Check it out—we have both ends of the spectrum on this list: from speculation, a form of investment that, like gambling, involves more risk-taking, to capital preservation. Money loses value over time. The only way we can preserve our capital's value is by using it to make more money through wealth-generating investments. Investing is also considered an income stream when the value of your shares increases and you sell them for a profit, as well as when you receive dividends from any dividend stocks. That profit and those dividends are both considered part of your income. This list only goes to show that you have the power to use the market to fit your individual needs. If the right option isn't speaking to you just yet, I suggest starting with growth. Once you've become a baller who needs to figure out how to preserve all your capital, feel free to update your objective.

After you've filled out the fields on the form, you will likely be asked to create a log-in and password, and voilà, you will have officially opened your very own brokerage account!

Logging into your account for the first time may feel overwhelming. There's a lot of information, and many of the words will likely still be quite unfamiliar. It's okay to feel this way. Don't let it scare you away. It's part of the process. Self-compassion is always required in new spaces, especially when hanging out in brokerage accounts and reviewing portfolios was not modeled in our lives. Take your time. As you begin to navigate your account, start connecting the terms we've discussed so far with what you see online. Go back to earlier chapters, and turn to the glossary on page 251 to continue familiarizing yourself with this new lingo. Look things up or do further research when curiosity bites, until this language starts to feel like second nature to you.

These are exciting times, you are embarking on a lifelong journey, and I know you may be lit with adrenaline and raring to go right into buying and selling. But the market ain't going nowhere, Warriors. We'll get to stock picking in the next chapter. Opening your brokerage account has opened the door into the stock market. Let's put in a quick doorstop so you can scout this new territory and gain some more ground before you charge in with guns blazing.

## GET TO KNOW THE TOP THREE INDEXES

Before we begin to actively participate in the stock market, it's essential to get a sense of its overall performance. We can't do this by tracking just one stock, so instead, we can take a look at the top three globally recognized US indexes we always hear mentioned in the news: the Dow Jones, the S&P 500, and Nasdaq. An **index** is a grouping of stocks that meet specific criteria to serve as a benchmark to track the movement of the market, allowing us to compare current price levels to past ones so that we can see the market's overall performance and measure the health of the economy. It's basically like an ongoing scoreboard that lets us know if a grouping of stocks has won or lost that day, week, quarter, or year.

These indexes were one of the first things I learned about and understood back in 2012 when I began researching the stock market while working at Netflix. It was the easiest way to keep track of the stock market without having to read a slew of articles on the topic. Once I began investing in 2013, I'd take a quick glance at my phone once the market closed for the day to see if those three indexes were green (up) or red (down). Then I'd check my investment to assess how it was doing in comparison. Before I get into how to understand these indexes in more depth, let's get to know them first, so you too can join investors across the map in using them as your go-to for key insights into the market.

The **Dow Jones Industrial Average**, most commonly known as the Dow or the Dow Jones, was created in 1896 by Charles

Dow and is the eldest of the top three indexes that measure our economy's health. It tracks thirty large, publicly owned blue chip companies, such as American Express, Coca-Cola, and Home Depot, which represent most major US market sectors and trade in the NYSE. The companies included in this index are considered market leaders in their trading sectors. (If you don't remember what blue chip stocks or market sectors are, go back to Step 3 for a refresher.)

The Dow is a price-weighted index, meaning it measures the price of shares as well as their fluctuation. Massive price changes in the market are reflected by the Dow and can be an indication of upward or downward movement in a specific sector. For example, it could show us that the technology sector is coming down and the energy sector is going up, which tells us tech is losing strength in our economy while oil and gas are gaining it. This, in turn, indicates that there's a transfer of money happening in those sectors, which illustrates how the economy may be shifting—that is, potentially growing stronger or weaker. A share with a higher price will have a bigger impact on the overall ups and downs of the Dow, but since the Dow is solely based on the price of the stock of large companies, it neglects to take into account smaller businesses, making it a skewed measurement of the overall US economy. In fact, many economists prefer to look at the S&P 500 to check the economy's temperature.

The **Standard and Poor's 500** index, also known as the S&P 500, was created in 1957. It measures the top five hundred largest and most important companies in the country. More companies means more accuracy in measuring the entire economy. The S&P

500 is a market capitalization–weighted index. While the Dow tracks the price of a share, the S&P 500 tracks the current **market capitalization** (a.k.a. market cap)—that is, a calculation of the worth of a company's total shares that is used to determine the company size. In essence, the Dow gauges the economy's health via share price fluctuations, while the S&P 500 measures health based on the value of a company. The companies included in this top five hundred list must continuously meet certain requirements to remain in this index—such as being headquartered in the United States and having a market cap of more than $6.1 billion. This means some companies with a mid market cap, which range in worth between $2 billion and $10 billion, and all companies with a small market cap, between $300 million and $2 billion, do not qualify. Based on these criteria, the list of companies in the S&P 500 is rebalanced every quarter. This is an index we pay extra-careful attention to because those five hundred companies have products or services that the majority of the US population consumes. So when this index is up or down, it is basically reflecting our consumer behavior and could be a clear indicator that our economy is heading in the right or wrong direction. Some S&P 500 mainstays include Apple, Johnson & Johnson, and General Electric. This index is a great benchmark for investors to get a sense of the market's "sentiment," which is finance language for how investors feel about a stock or the overall market.

The **Nasdaq Composite index**, a.k.a. the Nasdaq, specifically measures the stocks carried in the Nasdaq Stock Exchange (see Step 3, page 93), which means it tracks more than three thousand companies, most of which are based in the United States. This index was established by the National Association of Securities Dealers in 1971, which makes it the newest of the three major indexes. It is mostly recognized as a tech index, though it does hold a small percentage of other sectors. The Nasdaq, like the S&P 500, is also a market capitalization–weighted index, measuring the size fluctuations of the companies on this list—companies with a higher market cap will have more impact on these indexes—as well as how the tech sector is performing. Some companies included in this index are Amazon, Google, Microsoft, and Apple. As you can see, if a company, such as Apple, meets the requirements, it can be listed in more than one index, even all three.

Now that we know that indexes help us measure the health of the economy, how can we as investors use them to determine the health of our personal stock portfolio? Indexes can tell us how good or bad our portfolio is performing against a group of stocks. For example, when I started checking indexes, I paid close attention to the Nasdaq because when it was up, it was likely that Netflix stock was up, and vice versa. If Netflix was moving in the opposite direction of the Nasdaq, that told me something seriously negative or positive was happening with this particular stock, and it was my sign to dig deeper and read up on what was happening with Netflix on that particular day and why. Nowadays, I lean on the S&P 500 to check the market's health overall, since it tracks the top five hundred companies in the United States. I check the Nasdaq to see how tech is performing, since I have a tech-heavy portfolio. And I'll glance at the Dow for any major swings in leading companies within each sector, because if there are any, it could potentially tell me if investors may be readying themselves to leave one sector for another—say, from technology to energy stocks, which is one of the most common movements in the market. I usually check all three indexes at the end of each day, and I'll also take a midday peek if I want to get a quick temperature read on the market, but not everyone needs to do this on a daily basis. It will largely depend on the type of investor you want to be and your needs and goals. The most important thing is having a holistic view of what's happening in your portfolio and in the indexes.

## LEARN HOW TO READ AN INDEX CHART

Indexes are read in chart form. The line chart will give us red and green indicators on the line itself to highlight the upward or downward movement of the index. Green in the stock market always indicates a positive upward trend, while red indicates a downward trend. Charts for the three major indexes can be found in your brokerage account or through your favorite search engine by typing in the name of the index. Let's use the Nasdaq as our example here.

Go to Google and look up "Nasdaq index," then scroll to the line chart. Below the name of the index is the current level for Nasdaq, which as of today is 10,829.50. You will also see the numbers in point and percentage form telling us if the index is either up or down. Below the level is the chart's time frame, which usually ranges from one day (1D) to the maximum years available, going all the way back to when the Nasdaq was established and entered the market. This gives you an overall sense of how the value of Nasdaq has fluctuated within the current day, week, month, year, and more. Then there's a series of numbers under the chart that may vary slightly depending on your brokerage or search engine, but it usually includes the opening points—in other words, the level of the index at the start of traditional market hours that day—the highest and lowest points the index hit that day, and its fifty-two-week high and low.

---

### WEALTH WARRIOR TACTICS:
### *INDEX CHART POINTS VERSUS PERCENTAGES*

When you listen to your favorite news update or read the daily headlines, you will often see reporters open their finance segment by mentioning if the Dow was up or down that day or week. Index charts are usually analyzed using a points scoring system or a percentage system. Points and percentages are measurements used to identify how much the overall market has dropped or increased in a day or a week. On the daily, points in particular often fluctuate. And for newly minted retail investors, such as many of you, hearing that the Dow is down 215 points can sound terrifying, when, in fact, today that means it is down by only 0.69 percent. Points are basically converted into percentages to help put the numbers into perspective. They are one and the same, so to keep your cool on your Wealth Warrior journey, stick to using percentages to measure indexes.

# INHALE, EXHALE:
# WATCH THE MARKET BREATHE

The main point of checking the top three index charts on the regular is to determine how the market is performing—or, as I like to say, breathing. The stock market inhales on green days (when stocks go up) and exhales on red (when stocks come down). Becoming acquainted with these movements and why they happen will provide us with knowledge that has the potential to help us make balanced and informed moves instead of allowing our emotions to drive us to make rash decisions once we're actively participating in the market—an incredibly common reaction to entering the market, which we will explore in depth in Step 7. For now, let's get into the bulls and bears of it all.

### The Charging Bull

In 1987 the stock market dropped by 20 percent in one day—this was the steepest crash the market had ever seen in a twenty-four-hour period, and it came on the heels of a booming economic year. Because it happened on a Monday, this day in stock history became known as Black Monday. Inspired by this market crash, an Italian sculptor named Arturo Di Modica decided to sculpt a 7,100-pound, eleven-by-sixteen-foot bull. Di Modica had arrived in the United States penniless in 1970, and he felt indebted to the country because he was able to build a successful career there as a sculptor. When this masterpiece was finalized in December 1989, which is the year the market recovered to its pre-crash levels, he loaded it onto a truck, pulled up to the NYSE, and in true guerrilla art style, illegally dropped off the bronze sculpture on the sidewalk as a Christmas gift to his new country. Di Modica's intention was to inspire each person who encountered the bull to carry on fighting through the hard times after the 1987 stock market crash. He said, "My point was to show people that if you want to do something in a moment things are very bad, you can do it. You can do it by yourself. My point was that you must be strong."

The bull was temporarily impounded but has now become a permanent fixture in Downtown Manhattan and a Wall Street icon that draws thousands of tourists a day.

The use of *bull* in reference to the market—in this case the Dutch stock market, which was the first one in the world, founded in 1611, more than a hundred years before the start of the US stock exchange—came about in the early 1700s and was used to refer to a speculative purchase of a stock that was expected to rise in price. Now, taking the animal symbol into consideration, the bull *inhales* and charges, lifting its horns and breaking through whatever stands in its way, so a bull market represents the upward movement of the market, and a **bullish** investor is one who charges forward with faith that the stock market's uptrend will continue. So, for example, if the S&P 500 is up by 20 percent from the most recent low, with no sign of a downturn, then that is considered a **bull market**. Interestingly, unlike the Dow, which tracks thirty companies, or the Nasdaq, which can track more than three thousand companies but they're mostly in the tech sector, the S&P 500 is the only index used to measure if we are officially in a bull or bear market because it lists the top five hundred companies in the US economy, so it is a much broader snapshot.

Bull markets are exciting because investors make a lot of money across sectors, which you can tell by the increase in the price of stocks and the percentage increase in the S&P 500. They're also a sign of a healthy economy. The longest-running bull market in history spanned eleven years and ended when the COVID-19 pandemic struck in 2020.

## The Intimidating Bear

The bear stands tall, lifting its claws, and exhales a roar, shrinking anything that threatens it, representing the downward movement in the market, or a **bear market**. The actual term also came into use in the early 1700s, before the bull entered the picture, based on a proverb that warns we should not sell the bear's skin before we've caught it. A **bearish** investor retreats when they think the stock market is in a downtrend and will continue along that path. Many factors can contribute to a drop in the market, like changing geopolitical climates, such as Russia's escalated attacks on Ukraine that turned into an outright war; or a significant crisis, like COVID-19. While we cannot determine the length of time that we will be in a bear market, we can determine the severity of it, which depends on how low the market drops and how quickly.

The first sign of a possible bear market on the horizon is a **market correction**. This is when the whales, the sharks, and we tiny fish believe that a global or national event (like a war or a pandemic) could be bad for the economy and we begin to collectively sell off stocks in a wave, dropping the stocks' prices, and making the market decline more than 10 percent but less than 20 percent. This isn't bear territory yet, because the market still has the potential to recover and return to a bullish uptick if investors decide to buy up stocks again. As you can see, we have the collective power to move the market in one direction or another based on our sentiment about the economy and geopolitics. A correction is something we actually want to see take place more often than not because as stated in the name, it is correcting the market. In other words, it brings it back to lower levels after an uptrend, thus balancing it out and keeping it healthy. It's like breathing: we can't just inhale or exhale; we need to do both to stay alive. If the stock market is continuously inhaling and moving up and up, with no exhale in sight, we could potentially start heading toward a stock market bubble.

A **stock market bubble** happens when stock rises exponentially in value, most commonly over a short period of time, typically driven by investors' speculation. The bubble shown in the following figure is the 1999 tech bubble, when any company that had a dot-com in its name was being swooped up in a frenzy by investors because they speculated this was the next big thing in the market. You can see this in the rise of the line in the chart, which happened in the late 1990s. Many of these companies were startups that weren't bringing in any **revenue** and didn't even have a proper business plan, so when investors started realizing this, they began to drop their stocks like flies. The money stream dried up, and these companies immediately collapsed—the bubble burst, and it led to a market crash.

### Stock Market Bubble

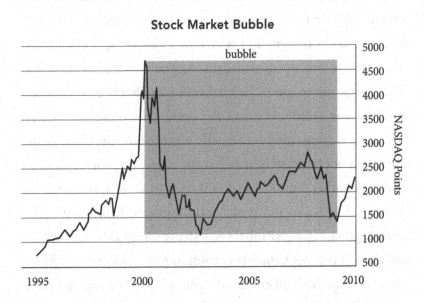

A **market crash** is determined when the S&P 500, which as mentioned earlier is the index we use to measure bear and bull markets, drops drastically, usually due to a major catastrophic event or the collapse of a speculative bubble. Famous stock market crashes include the 1929 Great Depression, Black Monday of 1987, the 2001 dot-com bubble burst, the 2008 financial crisis, and the 2020 COVID-19 pandemic. The latest crash began in January 2022. This sudden drop served as an indication that we were likely headed toward a bear market, which we officially entered on June 13, 2022, when the market dropped 20 percent.

When the market sustains a decline of 20 percent or more for two months—in other words, if a stock market crash persists for more than two months—we officially move from a market correction into a bear market. I know it may sound scary. But shit happens, and the market does crash from time to time. But historically it has gone up more than it's gone down, and it has recovered from every single crash.

Let this sink in. Since the 1950s the market has corrected twenty-six times and crashed eleven times. Sixteen of the twenty-six corrections averaged only fifty days. And ten of the eleven crashes averaged 391 days. Corrections keep the market healthy and crashes are inevitable, yet they also create great buy-in opportunities. Rather than fear the market correcting or crashing, which is to be expected, I'd be more worried about not participating at all.

Out of all the markers we use to gauge how the economy is going—from the real estate and job markets to inflation reports—the stock market is usually the first to drop, showing signals of trouble coming our way, and the first to begin making a recovery. This is because the stock market is forward looking. The numbers don't lie. Days between corrections or crashes dramatically outpace the days of the market's actual decline. For example, in 2008, the stock market hit bear market territory during the financial crisis, when the S&P 500 dropped by 48 percent in six months. The bottom lasted for seven days, from March 2 to March 9, then it started making a recovery. In other words, the market began recovering well before everything else in the economy.

The downs in the market may be for a short or longer stretch, but they're always temporary. Many of the investors who were in the market during the 2008 crash sold their shares and never returned, yet two years later the market had fully recovered, and it has been steadily rising since then (go to the S&P 500 chart online and click on "Max" to see the line chart indicating these movements). Rather than allowing the downs in the market to incite fear and panic-selling our stocks, Wealth Warriors work on being centered investors, so that we do not allow our emotions to get in the way of massive opportunities.

My personal experience and research on the history of the market during these last ten years has taught me that at the end of the day, what really matters is the amount of time you're in the market. If you're in it for the long haul, then withstanding a bear market is just like weathering a passing storm. The plus side is that it's also a time when you can buy into the market by purchasing stock at a lower price point—it's like getting a 20 percent discount or more—a move that could have you reaping the rewards for years to come! Knowing all this will help you navigate the ups and downs and the freak-outs you will feel when you first start learning how to breathe in the market yourself. Just remember: the sun will come out again, and with time, you will most likely end up earning more and losing less. That brings us to the next key element we need to define as we embark on this wealth-building journey.

## DETERMINE THE TYPE OF INVESTOR YOU WANT TO BE

Two investors with shares of the same company may have polar-opposite strategies and timelines. This doesn't make one person right and the other wrong; it just means their goals differ. To determine what type of stock market participant you want to become, it's important to understand the difference between a stock market investor and a stock market trader.

A **stock market investor** is a person who purchases shares and holds them for the long term with the expectation of generating profit. Stock market investors generally rely heavily on a fundamental stock analysis to help them decide whether a particular company would be a good investment opportunity. A **fundamental analysis** uses data like revenue, earnings, future growth, return on equity, profit margins, and more to determine the value of a company and its potential for future growth. We will get into more detail on this analysis in the next chapter.

A **stock market trader** is an investor who purchases and holds shares on a short-term basis—anything from minutes to days, weeks, or months. The trader depends on technical analysis to determine whether to buy or sell their stock. **Technical analysis** is the use of historical market data—including the price of a share and the volume, or the amount of people who are buying shares of a specific stock at a particular moment in time—to analyze stock charts and predict where a stock price is headed so that the trader can sell out of their shares and make a profit. Since their investments are mainly short term, stock market traders usually have minimal interest in a company's fundamentals. In short, being a trader is a full-time job, and one of the most stressful ones to boot.

If we were talking real estate, an investor would be someone who buys property and holds on to it for the long term, while a trader would flip the property for a profit and own it for only a short period of time. That's not what we're here for. We're not giving up our jobs to become traders; we're entering the market and learning how to use it to build long-term wealth for us and our future generations.

---

### WEALTH WARRIOR TACTICS:
### *LONG-TERM VERSUS SHORT-TERM INVESTMENTS*

A **long-term investment** is held for a year or longer, while a **short-term investment** is held for under a year. Short- and long-term investments are marked by your brokerage account at the time shares are sold. In other words, your brokerage will calculate and keep track of whether your investments were short or long term by looking at the time of sale of your stock. Your brokerage's online dashboard houses a document listing the sale of your assets and other transactions throughout the year that you can download and review.

Generally, long-term investors don't just hold their assets for one year, though—they aim to hold them without cashing out for a longer period of time, often more than ten or twenty years. In stock market speak, this is called a long-term investment horizon. Any asset held for less than five years is what we know as a short-term investment horizon. An investor with a long-term horizon is motivated by the potential growth that can come with time and is less worried about what may happen in the short term. Their goal is to make MONEY by giving it the time it needs to grow. The longer an investment is in the market, the more money you can potentially make, and the less risky your investment becomes.

## SET A TIME HORIZON

A **time horizon** is the length of time an investor expects to invest in an asset before cashing out. Identifying our time horizon when making an investment helps with navigating the emotions we may feel during volatile economic periods.

The economy is no placid lake; it will continuously shift, but with a long-term horizon, you have the freedom to not worry about the market's short-term ups and downs. Still, as a newbie, you will likely experience panic-driven heart palpitations when the economy takes a turn for the worse. That's okay. When that happens, remember these downturns in the stock market are short when compared to the rest of its timeline. Once you've recalled this key piece of information, reinforce your understanding that you and the business you are investing in are both in it for the long haul, unless something about the company changes and signals that you should exit that investment, which we will get to in Step 5. This is a slow-and-steady-wins-the-race kind of situation.

So, what kind of time am I talking when I say **long-term horizon**? I'd like you to commit to your stocks for at least five to ten years. The intention here is to give you the space to develop your inner investor while capitalizing on the power of time. Take renowned finance oracle Warren Buffett as an example. Just months after the 1987 Black Monday market crash, Buffett invested in Coca-Cola stock, which was $2.45 a share at the time. He has held on to those shares for thirty-five years and counting. As I'm writing this, each share is now worth $63.00 a pop. He owns four hundred million shares, has never sold a single one in all that time, and has said he has no plans to sell them in the near future either—the epitome of a long-term investment horizon. Volatile economic events have come and gone since his initial buy-in, but the passing of time has meant very minimal risk exposure compared to investments with **short-term horizons**, which are more exposed to what is happening in the economy and the current market. As of this moment, Buffett's Coca-Cola investment has made him $24.2 billion in gains alone, meaning this figure does not include the money he used to invest in his shares. Listen, there's no guarantee that Coca-Cola will remain above $2.45 forever; it could be disrupted by another beverage company one day, which could make the stock drop. Yet another advantage of being in this type of long-term investment is that if the stock does take a turn for the worse, an investor would begin to see the signs (which we'll discuss in Step 5) and have the chance to sell out of a position before their profits turn to major losses. To sum it all up, *more time equals less risk.*

I vividly remember a Netflix employee meeting where CEO Reed Hastings said that it isn't about what is happening now; it's about what will happen twenty years from now. By "it," he meant Netflix's operations and vision for growth, but this is the type of expansive thinking that will serve you when entering the market.

At the time, I believed that in approximately ten years, Netflix would be a much more mature company leading a streaming revolution. Additionally, at the rate the stock market was growing back then, I also felt confident that ten years would be the right amount of time to build the wealth I needed to purchase a house, which was the money intention I had set when I decided to enter the market. And I was hell-bent on sticking to this plan no matter what, unless I met this milestone sooner, of course. What I didn't realize was that I was basically committing to a long-term time horizon of ten years with my Netflix stock.

In the meantime, I had to manage my patience and keep the reasons why I felt so strongly about Netflix as an investment at the forefront of my mind. I reminded myself of the disruption that the company had already created from its inception and the potential it still had to change the way we consume media. Having this type of exposure to technology and getting to be a part of its operations team really informed the type of investor I am today. I do seek disruption and companies that are solving current challenges we are experiencing in the world today.

The thing is, in today's world of instant gratification, practicing the patience to wait it out one, five, or ten years can feel nearly impossible. When you have an investment in stocks, you also have a sell button staring back at you, tempting you to push it each time your money grows or you notice wavering in your gains. That's why emotionally detaching yourself from your money and investing only what you can afford to lose will potentially allow you to navigate the ups and downs of the market without making rash, emotional short-term decisions to the detriment of your long-term horizon.

I grew up experiencing constant change in my life, so a sense of stability was almost jarring. When I first started investing, I realized that each time my stock hit a hurdle or a standstill or it backpedaled, it fed into that voice in my head that pushed me to get out while I could. There goes that reticular activating system. I had to stand up to that voice and say, "Back off," but I was able to do that only because I had done my research and had a plan in place. That plan, to stick with Netflix for ten years, was mine to follow and mine to gain from. I was now beginning to honor time and embrace the idea that in life, not everything happens immediately. I eased off enough to not focus on the market as intently as I had done at the start of my journey, because it can become all-consuming, and that can be incredibly draining and unhealthy. Diligent research is good; fretting over the market every hour on the hour is not. I learned to let my investment do its thing, ride the waves, and breathe.

It's been ten years since I entered the stock market, and I am blown away by how one decision—to invest in the stock market—changed the course of my life. Today, I think of time in the market like the time you must put into something you truly want to master. You deserve to move with confidence in this space, to take calculated risks that pay off, and to stay the course when things get discouraging. Ten years from now, the stock market roller coaster will be one with familiar twists and turns. Till then, time and patience are key while your money works harder for you. Prepare for battle, Wealth Warrior—it's time to pick those stocks and enter this territory once and for all.

# STEP 5

# STOCK PICKING: INVEST IN WHAT YOU KNOW

If you ain't getting no pesos, ¿qué estás haciendo? Stack it up like Legos. Quiero dinero.

—*Jennifer Lopez*

Investing in the stock market is one of the greatest revolutionary acts that we can partake in as communities of color, not just to build our wealth but to incite change. Get this: according to the Federal Reserve, in 2021 the wealthiest 10 percent of Americans owned a record 89 percent of all US stocks. These are the keepers we're up against. If we want better corporations that offer higher-paying wages and equal opportunities, we not only have to create these types of companies but also have to become shareholders and supporters of the ones that already exist.

Choosing our stocks wisely, or stock picking, is our chance

not only to build our wealth and grow in the stock market but also to put our money where it matters. Shareholders essentially have the power to vote—by buying and selling stocks—on decisions made within companies. And it's true: companies usually care about their investors more than anything else because investors are the ones determining the value of the company. If a company disappoints its shareholders, they may decide to sell their shares, and this will lower the company's value by default. Additionally, the shareholders are the first ones to see the signs that a company is, let's say, unable to sustain itself. Consumers aren't usually paying attention to what a company is doing on a financial level—what its earnings are, how it's finding solutions to operational problems, and so forth. The shareholders and private investors are paying attention because their money depends on the company's good health. And that's why they get a vote in some of these decisions too. Keeping this in mind, imagine if the majority of a company's investors were people of color. Imagine the amount of voting power we'd have within a corporation. This would mean when we see something that's unaligned with our personal values, we'd have the voice and the means to signal that change is needed and usher in that change, leveling up both our financial and spiritual wealth.

## INVEST IN WHAT YOU KNOW

I once heard Warren Buffett say that owning shares in the stock market is like owning a piece of the United States. As if that isn't enough motivation, we have the right to participate and it's available to us all. The stock market is a place where prices of goods and services are determined by supply and demand that is created solely by buyers and sellers. If we go back to the grocery store, the government has no right to dictate what brand of beans we decide to buy; we have options, and if we can't find the brand we want in one store, we have the right to look for it elsewhere. Although I knew and understood this when I began buying shares, I still struggled to believe that investing was an option for me. Believing I needed to keep all my money in an emergency fund almost stopped me from moving it into my brokerage account. Not being white with blond hair and blue eyes, not having a finance degree, not feeling like I belonged, almost stopped me from demanding a spot in this bountiful arena. The fear of losing all my money almost stopped me from buying my first shares. But as an investor, I learned to look at what I was consuming to identify my right to participate in the market. In order to double down on your convictions and cancel the inner and outside noise, it's essential to invest in what you know. And all it takes is a quick look around.

Simply start by paying careful attention to your daily routine. Let's say you wake up to your Apple iPhone alarm and slide out of bed and into your Nike apparel for a quick free workout streaming on YouTube. Then you head out the door, grab a cold brew from Starbucks, and stop at Target for a few essentials before heading back home for a day of endless Zoom or Google Meet calls on your MacBook while streaming your favorite playlist on Spotify in between. Before the day is over, you check your

Microsoft Outlook inbox for any outstanding emails and open up your Microsoft 365 Word or Excel documents to plug in the info needed for tomorrow's report. Finally, after putting your dirty dinner dishes in the dishwasher you purchased at Home Depot, you unwind in the evening by binge-watching your favorite series on Netflix or choosing a family-friendly movie to stream on Disney+. Everything you use was produced by a company. And each one of these companies is making money off your consumption. What's more, if you look up your go-to brands for electronics, exercise gear, house appliances, and so forth, you will discover that many of them are produced by publicly traded companies.

An important part of investing is understanding the business you're investing in. By no means should you invest in Apple, Starbucks, Microsoft, Disney, and Netflix at the same time right out of the gate. But you do already have a head start with the products you consume regularly and are familiar with—that's an automatic launching pad for choosing which stocks to start investing in. Grab a notebook or open your Notes app, and start a list of all the brands you love and use day in and day out. Then narrow down that initial list by looking them up online to see if they are private or publicly traded companies. Remember: only publicly traded companies have stocks available for purchase in the market. Once you have a list of publicly traded companies that produce the products you use, it's time to get familiar with the business side of the company as well as the person who runs it and their plans for its future, ten or twenty years from now.

In the summer of 1937, when Warren Buffett, who now has a net worth of more than $96 billion, was only seven years old, he began to observe how every evening, like clockwork, people would head out to their lawns to cool off from the day's heat. At that time, air-conditioning was not yet a thing. A light bulb went off in this little boy's mind: maybe he could sell cold soda pop to his neighbors, who were craving anything that might refresh their heat-exhausted bodies. First, he collected the bottle caps piled up at the bottom of the bottle openers mounted on soda pop coolers at the local gas stations. He spent weeks gathering these caps, and after sorting them, he learned that Coca-Cola sales in his hometown far exceeded the sales of any other pop. This was his market research. Buffett's grandfather owned a grocery store, so they negotiated a deal on the purchase of Cokes. Buffett began selling the pop to his neighbors and created quite a profitable business. By the time he was eleven years old, in 1941—and through the support of modeled behavior from his father, who had a brokerage firm, and grandfather, who owned his own business—Buffett had bought his first three shares in the stock market, but not of Coca-Cola, which had become a publicly traded company in 1919. Buffett did not become a Coca-Cola investor until 1988, and he still jokes about not investing in this company he knew so well sooner.

As Buffett demonstrated at a mere seven years old, you don't have to be an expert to see trends taking place in your daily life. He also showed us that when we have an inkling of what to buy early on, we shouldn't ignore that feeling—he probably could've made millions more had he started buying Coca-Cola shares before 1988. Still, if you do take more time to get to that point of buying in, that's okay too—hey, it took me thirty-two years to enter the market, and I have no shame in that. This all goes to show that each person's wealth-building journey will be different. For that reason, I'm not here to hand out fish or tell you what to buy; I'm here to teach you how to fish, to empower you to choose the stocks that are right for you. In order to do that, we must go beyond participating in a company's growth with our consumer behavior and learn how to further assess and develop our own perspectives in this financial space to make sound and steadfast decisions that will impact our wealth.

## LET'S GET TECHNICAL: STOCK CHART BASICS

This section may feel tedious because some of it will sound similar to the index chart basics we've already reviewed. I know you've already digested those pages and you feel revved up and ready to go, but stay with me, because this info here will arm you with the knowledge you need to potentially succeed in the market. Let's go back to the charts we began to analyze a few pages earlier, but now, instead of pulling up index charts, let's look at a company's chart. I'll use Apple as an example to guide you through this process and show you the technical tools and signals that will help support your investment journey. This type of analysis can flag great buy-in opportunities and help you steer clear of investment moves that may not be beneficial for you or could even cause trouble. I really enjoy having this type of information within reach, because it not only feeds me valuable know-how but also helps me through my emotional journey in the market by giving me the awareness needed to be more confident in my long-term investments and goals.

Go to Google on your computer or phone and search for your stock. In this case, type "Apple stock chart" in the search bar. (Note: make sure you include the term "stock" in your search so that what you have on-screen matches what we're about to describe.) The information you see on the page is gathered by Google Finance. The first thing you will notice at the top is the company's full name—in this case, Apple Inc.—along with its ubiquitous logo, which will assure you that this is indeed the company you want to research. Under the company's name, you will see "NASDAQ: AAPL." This means that Apple pertains to the Nasdaq index, and AAPL is its ticker symbol. A **ticker symbol** is a unique series of three to five letters assigned to a publicly traded security so that it can be traded on an exchange, similar to when a cashier punches in a code at the grocery store register to identify your fresh produce. You use ticker symbols to look up companies so you can buy or sell stock or simply review their charts.

Next to the company's name and ticker symbol, you will see "Overview," "News," "Compare," and "Financials." We will be focusing on the company's overview, but if you click on "News," you will get current news regarding the company; if you go to "Compare," you'll get a list of other publicly traded companies in the same sector or closely related sectors that you can compare Apple with; and if you hit "Financials," you will have access to the company's financial information.

A **stock chart** tracks a stock's price over a certain time frame.

The big number above the chart is the stock's current price. On the day and time I checked Apple's stock chart for this example, it was trading at 138.88 USD—that is, $138.88. The price will show up in red when it's actively coming down from a higher price point and green when it's actively going up; if there is no movement, it will remain black. Right below the price is a figure and percentage within parentheses, followed by an arrow and the word "today." This indicates the change in price and percentage for the day. On this day, the stock was down by $6.15, or 4.24 percent. If you happen to look up a chart after regular market hours have closed, then the price information you will see in this area of the chart will reflect the previous day's price and percentage.

The chart itself is called a stock line chart, which tracks stock price levels over moments in time. It's made up of a series of data points called markers that are connected by straight-line segments. The price range is on the vertical axis, and the actual time of day is on the horizontal axis. The dotted line in the middle of the chart shows us where the stock closed on the previous day—in this case, $145.03. Like index charts, stock charts also show the time frame at the top. Say you want to see how Apple has performed for more than the last twenty-four hours. Simply click on "5D," "1M," "6M," "YTD," "1Y," or "5Y" to check how it did the previous week, months, and years. If you click on "Max," you'll get to see its overall lifetime performance since the moment it entered the stock exchange. For every time frame, if you place your cursor or finger on the chart you've pulled up and move it left or right, you will see the exact price points and the date and time the stock hit each price point.

On the day I checked the Apple stock chart for this example, its stock had gone up by $95.21 (218.02 percent) within the five-year time frame. Based on the percentage, this means that if you had invested in Apple five years ago, your money would have doubled its value! What savings account will give you that type of return on your cash? Hold up—I'm not saying that you should take all your money out of your savings account and deploy it in the market. That would defy the rule of investing only what you can afford to lose. All I want is for you to see the importance of having the tools to understand the market while participating in this type of investment. What's more, these figures do a great job of highlighting the type of growth that can take place for long-term investors when we are patient and allow the stock to rise.

I want you to take a quick break right now to carefully chew and digest what you've read so far until it goes from feeling foreign to feeling familiar and inspiring. It's like when we move to a new neighborhood and step into the local grocery store for the first time—we have no clue where our favorite items are, so we need time and a few visits to get our bearings, but it's also exciting to explore this new spot. Eventually, we will learn to navigate those aisles as if we've been there all along. That's what will happen in the stock market too. As I have said before and will continue to remind you, be patient and compassionate with yourself. It takes time, but you will get there. Okay, ready? Let's soldier on now and learn about the other, more technical information that sits below the chart.

## Market Capitalization

Market capitalization, as we've seen in earlier chapters, refers to the total value of the company's shares of a stock. This is calculated by multiplying the total number of shares by the present share price. For example, a company with twenty million shares selling at $100 each has a market cap of $2 billion. This data point is already calculated for us and listed as a quick reference next to the heading "Mkt cap" below the stock's line chart. Note that this number changes when the company's share price increases or decreases. Apple's market cap when I last checked while writing these pages was 2.21T ($2.21 trillion). We look to this figure to identify if the stock we are interested in is large cap, mid cap, or small cap.

✓ **Large cap stocks** are companies with market capitalizations of $10 billion or more. They are considered safer investments based on their reputation and ability to sustain growth. Most blue chip stocks are large cap. (See Step 3, pages 100–106, for a refresher on categories of stocks.)

✓ **Mid cap stocks** are companies with market capitalizations between $2 billion and $10 billion. They are considered a riskier investment but have the potential and room for future growth. Companies with mid cap stocks may not be the leaders of their industry, but they may be working toward achieving that status.

✓ **Small cap stocks** are companies with a market capitalization between $300 million and $2 billion and are considered the riskiest investments of all because their longevity and profitability are less set in stone.

As you identify what stocks you want to invest in, it's important to note what their market capitalization is and where they fall in these categories. It's one of the data points that will help you understand what type of investment you hold if you're an active investor—when you "hold" a stock in your portfolio, you're usually a long-term investor in it—or what type of investment you want to potentially hold if you're a new investor. Think of it this way: the more people consume a product, the safer it is in the stock market. That's why Nike is more stable than Lululemon, for example. As a new Wealth Warrior investor, you will want to invest in companies that are less volatile, companies that will provide you with some sort of stability in their price fluctuation and earnings.

## Price-to-Earnings Ratio

The **price-to-earnings (P/E) ratio** is one of the most fundamental ways old-school Wall Streeters evaluate the value of a publicly traded company, as well as value investors, who focus on picking stocks that are priced for less than their book value, which is a company's net difference between its total assets and total liabilities. This data point is calculated by dividing the company's current stock price by its current earnings per share. (For more on EPS, see pages 177–180.)

Typically, P/E ratios are measured against the S&P 500. The average ratio on the S&P 500 is 15, a historical benchmark for many value investors. If a company has a 15 P/E ratio, this means it is trading at 15 times its earnings per share. A 15 or lower P/E ratio is considered to be a cheap or inexpensive stock price. If the P/E ratio is high, then the stock price is considered expensive. However, not every company with a low P/E is a good investment, and not every company with a high P/E is a bad investment. Many value investors will not invest in stocks with a high P/E ratio, which for some may equal 15 or more, but for others may mean 20 and above, while other investors consider P/E ratios an outdated metric. Interestingly, companies such as Google, Amazon, Tesla, and Netflix, to name a few, all had incredibly high P/E ratios, which kept many investors away from purchasing these stocks, causing them to miss out on incredible high-performing investments.

This data point can get pretty tricky—it should never be the only piece of information you look at when making a decision on an investment, but it's important that we are aware of our stock's P/E ratio and understand what it means.

## Dividends

If the company pays out a dividend (see Step 3, pages 102–103, for a refresher on dividend stocks), then the stock chart will provide you with a dividend yield ("Div yield"). If not, that area will remain blank. The **dividend yield** is the ratio of the current stock price to the total dividend amount over the last year. In other words, it is the percentage that is being paid out as a dividend according to the stock price. Apple's current dividend yield is 0.66 percent. This gives you a sense of how much you can make from a particular stock. It is great to find companies that have a high dividend yield if this is part of your investment strategy, but it is important to note that a high dividend yield is not always a good sign, as it could mean that the stock price has declined significantly. Remember to take a look at what's going on with the company overall to see where you should invest your money.

## The CDP Score

A **CDP score** is given to companies by a nonprofit organization (formerly known as the Carbon Disclosure Project) that assesses and discloses their environmental impact. By scoring companies on a standardized scale, it aims to prevent dangerous climate change and environmental damage by informing investors how publicly traded companies are affecting the environment. This is based on an assessment of information that the companies voluntarily disclose. Much like school grades, the score ranges from A to F, with A being the best score. This allows us investors to choose companies that align with our beliefs regarding the protection of the environment. Continuing with our Apple example, it currently has an A-minus.

## The Fifty-Two-Week High and Low

The **fifty-two-week high** (see the "52-wk high" heading on a stock's chart) indicates the highest price point the share has reached and closed at within the last fifty-two weeks, while the **fifty-two-week low** ("52-wk low") indicates the lowest price point the share has traded and closed at in the last fifty-two weeks. The fifty-two-week high and low can help us identify good buy-in opportunities—for example, if the current price of a share is closer to the low number.

---

Learning how to read stock charts will help you see the company you are researching on a more technical level. It will also make you feel more confident when you look up a chart, because you'll know what all that stock market jargon actually means. Knowledge is truly power. Nevertheless, please note that some of the more detailed numbers tracked in these charts, like the P/E ratio and market cap, should not be your main points of reference as a new investor when deciding whether a company is worth your money. I urge you to always do your homework and gather as much information as you can about your potential investments beyond the info you now know how to interpret from a stock chart. That's just the tip of the iceberg. Look into a company's products (which you'll already be familiar with if you're choosing a company that produces items you use), trends, CEO, and most importantly, financial statements, which I will show you how to read next. These statements will let you know if a company can sustain itself financially, so make sure not to skip this; it should be your bread and butter when it comes to responsibly picking your stocks.

## READ FINANCIAL STATEMENTS

By law, publicly traded companies are required to report their financial statements. This law is regulated by the SEC.

There is an annual report known as the 10-K, as well as a quarterly report known as the 10-Q. The 10-K report provides in-depth financial information that has been audited. The 10-Q report provides unaudited financial information that is ongoing, along with company updates.

The quarterly financials are what investors typically focus on, as they tell us what is taking place with publicly traded companies throughout the year. There are four quarters in each year, and therefore, reports are made public four times a year, which are known as **earnings seasons**. For the most part, earnings season begins one to two weeks after the last month of each quarter. So quarter one (Q1) is January through March, and Q1 earnings season begins in early to mid-April. Q2 is April through June, and Q2 earnings season begins in early to mid-July. Q3 is July through September, and Q3 earnings season begins in early to mid-October. Q4 is October through December, and Q4 earnings season begins in early to mid-January.

The 10-K and 10-Q reports are each broken down into three sections, which are referred to as financial statements: a balance sheet, an income statement, and a cash flow statement. These are accounting reports that summarize the activity that is taking place in the business every quarter. So while looking at the stock charts is more of a technical analysis to see how a stock is behaving day to day, checking these three financial statements will help you assess the company's fundamental analysis, which is like looking at a company's résumé.

## The Balance Sheet

The balance sheet is the statement that we are going to analyze the most, as it has high-level information that can provide us with key indicators when assessing potential investments. It shows us the financial strength of the company and provides us with a snapshot of the company's assets and liabilities, as well as its shareholders' equity, within a moment in time. For example, if you were to check your bank account and your credit card transactions as of today, you would see specific numbers pertaining to the current activity taking place in your accounts. In your savings and checking accounts, you would find line items where money is leaving your account and line items where money is entering your account. On your credit card statement, you will find line items that reflect your expenses and how much money is due. This is similar to what we will review when looking at a balance sheet; it's a snapshot of the company's money coming in and going out. Note that balance sheets will look different from company to company, as the nuances in the line items pertain to the type of business that they are in. For example, Starbucks' inventory will be different from Apple's inventory.

The **balance sheet** provides information on what a company owns, how much it owes, and how it was funded. It represents an accounting equation (Assets = Liabilities + Shareholders' Equity) through the data it provides, which must literally balance, or be equal, hence the name *balance sheet*.

There are several places where you can access a company's financial statements. While I do like using Google Finance for a quick search of the charts and easy access to information at the bottom of the charts, which we previously reviewed, I prefer Yahoo Finance for the fundamental information. That said, it is important that you not get overwhelmed with the overload of information the website provides, so I'm keeping the explanation here beginner-friendly, covering only the essential information you need for now.

Enter the ticker symbol you want to research on Yahoo Finance, and you will see the company profile. Click on "Financials," which is one of the menu tabs right above the stock chart. That will take you to the company's financials. Now click on "Balance Sheet." At the top right corner above the sheet, you have the option to look at the quarterly or annual reports. Click on "Annual." This is very helpful when doing research for a company for the very first time, prior to purchasing the stock, because it will give you a snapshot of the company's last four years. This is also an audited snapshot, which is why it is good to look at this first when assessing if this is a company you want to invest in. Once you become an actual shareholder, looking at quarterly reports for ongoing information will be more beneficial than reading annual reports. As a reminder, the stock price will make most of its drastic moves either up or down when quarterly reports are released, unless there's any big news on the company, which can also be a **catalyst** for movement on the stock price.

The balance sheet is broken down into five sections: current assets, non-current assets (long-term assets), current liabilities, non-current liabilities (long-term liabilities), and shareholders' equity. Note that all the numbers are scaled by the thousands, which means that though the figures look like they are in millions, they are actually in billions. In other words, add three zeros to get the real value. Let's break down the sections to help you identify key factors that indicate how a company is doing.

First up are total assets. Assets are everything a business owns that has monetary value and is used to generate profits. Total assets, which include current assets and non-current assets, are the total amount of that monetary value. Assets are always listed in order of liquidity. Liquidity is direct cash on hand. The order of liquidity is how fast the company can access its cash—some assets are not cash on hand, but they can be converted into cash. When determining the value of a company, it is important to understand how many assets are immediately available and how many will take some time to liquidate, or turn into cash.

Contrary to non-current assets, which are accessible only after a year, current assets include cash; stocks (yes, businesses also invest their money in stocks!), which can easily be converted to cash; and other assets that are expected to be converted to cash within a year.

Liabilities include anything that the company owes or has borrowed and eventually has to pay to other parties. Just like with assets, the liabilities are broken down into two sections: current liabilities, which are due to be paid within one year; and non-current liabilities—also known as long-term liabilities—which are due at any point after one year.

The last section in the balance sheet that I want you to pay attention to is **shareholders' equity**, which is its assets minus its liabilities and represents the company's net worth. If the company produces a profit for the year, then that money or net income (assets minus liabilities) flows into shareholders' equity. Once the year closes, the shareholders' equity is known as **retained earnings**. Retained earnings can be kept on the balance sheet, or they can be paid out to shareholders in the form of dividends. If the company produces a loss, this means that it incurred more liabilities than income on the balance sheet, and this would either put the retained earnings as a negative or lower the existing retained earnings from the previous year.

Ultimately the balance sheet is letting us know the current state of profitability of a company. There are many ways that financial analysts look at financial statements. For now, we are covering the basics. As your journey matures, so will this process.

Now it's time to put it all together. Look at the annual balance sheet, and check if the total assets have been increasing year over year. It is positive to see assets increase year over year and could be alarming to see them decline or fluctuate. However, we need to take into consideration the time that the company has been in business. For younger companies, it takes awhile to see assets increase, since they may not be profitable yet or they could be reinvesting all their money into equipment, top-tier talent, and so forth. Or perhaps something happened on a macro level that affected their sector. A great example of this was airline companies during the start of the pandemic, when nobody was flying—quarterly earnings were affected because they were not selling many tickets and bringing in revenue. This will, in turn, affect overall annual earnings. However, this was something that was out of the company's control. We have to take factors like these into consideration.

Now look at the company's total liabilities. Are those also increasing year over year? While it may seem like a negative to see liabilities increase year over year, it is not as negative as you may think. Remember: it takes money to make money, and the cost of running a business is far from zero, so if a company isn't taking on liabilities, it is likely not reinvesting in itself. Therefore, seeing liabilities increase year over year can be a positive thing, especially if assets are also increasing yearly. It can be more concerning when liabilities are continuously outpacing assets, especially for a mature company. This may signal deeper issues pertaining to the company's overall profitability. What if liabilities are decreasing year over year? Incremental decreases can be a positive signal that the company is becoming more efficient in its operations. But if their liabilities are decreasing drastically, that could be a bad sign because we need to see companies leveraging money and putting it to work.

When it comes to equity, it's great to see it increase year over year, as that means more retained earnings or more profit sharing will come to us as investors in the form of dividends. However, this is all going to depend on how the company is performing with their assets and liabilities.

Another great way to draw conclusions from the balance sheet is through an equation known as **current ratio**, which is calculated by dividing the current assets by the current liabilities. We take the current numbers, because these are liquid assets that are accessible in less than a year, as well as current liabilities, which are due to be paid in less than a year. The current ratio lets us know the health of the business and how long it could sustain itself if the business had to shut down. A great example of this was early on in the pandemic when some businesses were not able to operate and everything had to come to a complete stop.

Let's calculate the current ratio for Alphabet Inc., also known as Google, the darling of balance sheets. To get this number as close to current as possible, we need to look at the most recent quarterly balance sheet versus the annual balance sheet. Alphabet's current assets at the time of writing this book are $172,371,000 (remember that this number shows up in thousands on Yahoo Finance, but the ratio stays the same whether you add the three zeros or not). Its current liabilities are $61,354,000.

$$172,371,000,000 / 61,354,000,000 = 2.81$$

If the current ratio is greater than one, then the company's assets exceed its liabilities, which is a good thing because it means the company is able to pay off its existing liabilities. In this case, Alphabet is able to pay off its liabilities almost three times over. In other words, it is in great health financially and could sustain its business in the event of a shutdown. Banks like to lend money to businesses that have a ratio that ranges between one and two. If the ratio is greater, you may think it's a great thing; however, this presents a different perspective on the company, in that it may not be reinvesting in itself to help further its growth. Again, it takes money to make money, and banks as well as investors want to see that companies are using their money to make more money and it is not just sitting there. This is something that we can apply to the way we use our own money: Are we using it to make more money via investing, or are we simply just keeping it in a savings account?

If a company's ratio is less than one, then its assets are less than its liabilities. This is a negative, as it lets us know that the company is unable to pay liabilities or money owed in full.

Overall, the current ratio, along with the comparison year over year of the balance sheet, gives us key indicators of how the company is performing. We can use these numbers to compare the company with other leaders in the same sector or industry peers to see how it stacks up.

## The Income Statement

While the balance sheet gives us a snapshot of a company at a specific point in time, the **income statement**, also known as a profit and loss statement, will show us the company's revenue, which is money generated from goods and services; **cost of goods sold (COGS)**, which tells us the cost of producing the goods or services sold; and expenses, including any operational costs to run the business, over a period of time. While a part of the balance sheet reflects how much cash is on hand, the income statement shows us how the company got that cash on hand. It gives us insight that will help us to see the company's performance and ultimately how it reached the cash in its assets, and the expenses in its liabilities line items on the balance sheet. Ultimately, the income statement lets us know the company's profit by reflecting how it's performing in generating revenue and how efficient it is with operating expenses.

The company's profit is broken down into three sections: **gross profit**, which is revenue minus COGS; **operating profit**, or EBIT (earnings before interest and taxes), which is gross profit minus operating expenses; and **net income**, which is operating profit minus interest and taxes. This final calculation gives us the total amount of profit that is free and clear of all costs and expenses.

Many times when you hear businesspeople discuss the profitability of a business, like on *Shark Tank*, this question comes up: What is the top line of the company, and what is the bottom line? The **top line** is how much revenue has come into the company, and the **bottom line** is the net income—again, all the money that is free and clear of costs and expenses.

When comparing this statement quarter over quarter and year over year, we can see how efficient or inefficient and how profitable or unprofitable a business has become. This is helpful when comparing industry peers, but it shouldn't be used to compare different business models because the line items will look different. Let's say you want to invest in companies that have a very similar business model, like Walmart and Target—this may be a statement you would want to explore to compare the companies' business models' efficiency and profitability. In keeping this analysis beginner-friendly, the most important part of this statement is the profitability. We will take a closer look at how profits are analyzed when we review earnings per share on page 177.

## The Cash Flow Statement

The **cash flow statement** reports how much money is flowing in and out of the company during a period of time. Investors review this statement on a quarterly or annual basis. While the income statement reflects how much profit a company is making, the cash flow statement gives us a deeper understanding of what is happening with a company's cash, which is ultimately what is needed for a company to operate and pay for its expenses, cost of goods, investor dividends, and so forth. Without cash there's no business; for this reason, the cash flow statement is considered one of the most important statements we can use to take a closer look at where the cash on hand listed on the balance sheet is coming from. Many companies fail because more cash is flowing out than flowing in.

The cash flow statement is split into three main sections: cash from operations, as in money that is coming in from products and services; cash from investment activities, which is money coming in from assets and investments the company may be making (commercial real estate is an example of a common investment); and cash from financing activities, which is money coming from debt and equity financing. This last one was a little hard for me to grasp initially because we are so accustomed to being taught that debt is bad, but, as discussed earlier, in business a reasonable amount of debt is not necessarily bad; it is simply leverage to make a business happen and ultimately an investment that has the potential to lead to more money. When a company borrows money, that money is counted in its cash line items on the balance sheet as an asset. The cash that comes from investments and from financing is not counted as a company's profit, which makes our definition of *cash* more expansive.

When checking this statement, see if the cash flow of the company is positive or negative. If the cash flow is positive, it does not necessarily mean that the company is profitable. Remember that cash does not equal profits. What a positive cash flow does signal is that a company can pay its debts and reinvest in the business, which is a good thing. If the cash flow is negative, it does not mean that the company is not profitable, but it can mean that the company is spending more than it is earning, which can be a bad thing. It can also mean that the company is simply reinvesting in its business and paying off debt or dividends, which can be a good thing. The objective is simply to see how much cash a company is actually generating from its business and how it is spent during a period in time. For many analysts, the cash flow statement is key because it gives clear insight into the true profitability of the business and if it can sustain itself.

At the end of the day, all three of these statements work together to provide us with a high level of understanding of a company's financial health. For me, understanding these nuanced statements also put into perspective how money is an instrumental tool and how my relationship with it affects the way I manage my finances in both my professional and my personal life.

Along with the financial statements, every quarter, a company shares a press release and an earnings call to not only summarize its financial statements but also provide its latest news, updates, and guidance. Once you've wrapped your head around financial statements, it's time to dive into earnings calls.

---

**WEALTH WARRIOR TACTICS:**
*THE INVESTOR RELATIONS PAGE*

When you become an investor in a company, you should immediately head over to the investor relations page on their website, which is usually found at the very bottom of their site. If you don't see it there, do a quick search using the company's name and "investor relations" and the page should be the first one to show up on the list of results. On the investor relations page, you will have access to the company's financial statements and earnings calls. Most will also have an investor newsletter that provides key information investors should be aware of and includes alerts about where

> you can find the company's latest earnings calls. This information is distributed in different ways depending on the company. Your brokerage account will also inform you of upcoming earnings calls and where to access those specifically pertaining to your investments, but signing up for information on each company's investor relations page will guarantee you receive relevant information directly from each business.

## LISTEN UP: QUARTERLY EARNINGS CALLS ARE HELLA FIRE

Industry professionals will have an opinion on what stocks you should choose, but having an opinion doesn't necessarily make them right. When I first started buying stock, my level of conviction wasn't based on intuition; it was based on the diligent research I executed on my investment. So when people said that I should sell my Netflix stock while I had the chance, I didn't. Why? Because I knew my shit on this company—how they were shifting consumer behavior and their potential for market share—which gave me the strength to overcome my system's external pressure. My knowledge was my shield—it gave me the power to defend my position. Dealing with that pressure can be difficult; it's like facing bows and arrows and machetes wielded by industry professionals who have more experience than you.

We have to hold our shields up to protect ourselves from everyone else's fears and scarcity mindsets. When you have done your research and understand the company you are investing in, no attack will sway you. So grab your list of publicly traded companies, and let's get to work, Wealth Warriors.

Earnings season takes place on a quarterly basis. During this time, companies are required to submit their income statements, cash flow statements, and balance sheets to the SEC. Shortly after the release of these statements, the company distributes a press release explaining the numbers on the statements and conducts a conference call during which executives discuss the quarterly results and answer questions from investors and analysts—a.k.a. the **earnings call**. The second time I heard a quarterly earnings call for Netflix, I realized that everything Reed Hastings had talked about at our employee meeting a week or so earlier was now being shared on the company's call. That meant the public was privy to the same knowledge we had as employees. In other words, you don't have to work for the company you want to invest in to find out its current circumstances and future projections and plans; all you have to do is listen to these damn calls. That's where companies lay out their financial results for the previous quarter and their plans for the upcoming months and years for anyone to process and scrutinize.

When I started taking these quarterly earnings calls seriously and tuning in, it was as if one minute I was placidly floating in a pool on a hot summer's day, and the next I was frantically splashing over to the ledge and holding on for dear life, realizing I didn't know how to swim well enough to handle the deep end. Eventually, I learned how to doggy-paddle my way through these calls by pausing the recording every few minutes to write down the words or phrases I didn't understand. Soon I felt as if I were learning how to do the butterfly like nobody's business. These calls gave me the chance to listen to renowned CEOs such as Tim Cook from Apple, Jack Dorsey from Block, and Safra Catz from Oracle talk about where their companies were right then and where they were headed. We get to hear the people who are essentially facilitating our day-to-day lives give us forward guidance on what they've created and their growth plans in real time. They also give invaluable insight into how and why stock prices are affected by earnings calls. Funnily enough, earnings season calls are now one of my favorite experiences as a stock market investor. In fact, if I were a business professor, I would make them mandatory for my students. I know, you're probably thinking I'm nuts. These calls can initially feel overwhelming, tedious, and downright long. But there is no better way to understand a business on a higher level than to listen in on earnings calls—they hold the key to a company's future projections. Once you learn this language and understand what is being communicated, you can use it to finish building your case for or against a particular stock by evaluating whether it aligns with who you are and what you want.

The most anticipated number during quarterly earnings seasons, the one that has investors and company execs on the edge of their seats, is the **EPS, earnings per share**. The EPS will help us to compare the profitability of different companies, even though every company will have different profit and share amounts. EPS is a fair comparison, as it tells us how profitable a company is per share. A high EPS tells us the company is generating more profits per share. EPS is calculated by dividing the net income of a company by its outstanding shares—that is, the amount of shares the company has issued for distribution/ownership. Alone, the net income reflects the company's overall income as if we the investors were the sole owners; this is not a great indication of how our investment shares are performing. What we want to look at is the earnings the company has per share and how that increases or decreases for the shares we actually hold. This is going to give us a clear indication of the profitability of each share we own or intend to own. For example, let's compare Target and Walmart. Target reported $31 billion in gross profit for 2021, and Walmart reported $143 billion in gross profit in the same year. Just by looking at gross profit, you might think that Walmart is much more profitable. However, when we calculate the EPS, Target is profiting $8.83 per share, while Walmart is profiting $5.00 per share. This tells us that although Walmart made a higher gross profit, it is making lower profits on a per-share basis. In this case, Target produces more profits per share. Analysts release their companies' expected EPS based on their most recent income statements. Then the companies reveal the actual EPS once the income statement is released and the EPS is calculated from the profit reported. This EPS is measured against the estimated number to see if it met, beat, or missed analyst expectations.

Every quarter is an opportunity for the company to learn from the last, measuring not just against itself but in comparison to other publicly traded companies. So we as investors don't want to just look at the numbers; we want to find the reasons behind the numbers. Think of it as following your favorite Olympic runner throughout their career. This is an athlete whose previous results, injuries, weaknesses, strengths, times, and medals are all carefully logged. Both the runner and dedicated fans of the sport can create a projection based on the runner's past performance to determine the time they have to meet or beat in their next race. That's exactly what's happening with publicly traded companies as they work to meet or beat their EPS. If a company beats earnings expectations, the company will be rewarded (investors will purchase more shares, which will drive its stock price up); if it misses this target, the company will be scrutinized by investors and analysts, as it may be an indication of more severe problems. Shares will likely be sold, driving the stock price down. Investors typically step in to buy more shares or sell existing ones based on this data point. That's why we tend to see the biggest jumps in stock price during earnings season.

The release of a company's financial statements, earnings calls, and press releases will further inform you of the "why" of a company's EPS. This is where the company will take the time to explain what took place with its quarterly earnings. If it missed its estimated EPS, it may go on to explain it was a supply chain issue or something that was completely out of its control, which would let you know that it wasn't due to mismanagement of the company itself. If it surpassed its estimated EPS, this gives it a chance to share what improved and why. Always make sure to keep your ears tuned to info that will impact your investment in a positive or negative way.

Last but not least, we want to look for forward guidance from the company during its earnings calls. If it's developing new products or services, for example, then this may indicate a growth opportunity, which is a great sign. Keep these questions in mind: Is the company growing its markets? Are its financial statements healthy? Is the balance sheet showing growth quarter after quarter, year after year? Is the company taking risks to expand into new markets (increasing liabilities responsibly)? Is it making life-changing products that leave a generational impact? However, there are times when companies are not able to provide forward guidance. We saw this a lot during the beginning of the COVID-19 pandemic, when it was challenging to perceive what would happen, with country-wide shutdowns and massive amounts of people getting sick. We must home in on the details but never lose sight of the bigger picture, especially in the global economy we now live in.

Remember: this is a spiritual and emotional journey as much as it is a financial one. The emotions evaluating each stock stirs up in you will let you know if as an investor you may potentially feel more at ease with growth stocks or cyclical stocks, safer or riskier categories. If the idea of investing in a hot stock like Tesla tightens up your chest, then maybe you're better off investing in a less disruptive and more stable company like Coca-Cola. Don't let anyone bully you into purchasing stock that makes you feel uneasy just because it's popular or lucrative at the moment. And don't allow your emotions to hold you back either—56 percent of millennial women say fear stops them from investing. Change that statistic by moving forward in your generational wealth-building journey and choosing what aligns with you, your needs, and your money intentions. You'll sleep better at night. Ultimately, what we must look for in these calls are reasons to back our investment convictions and why they continue to align with our intentions and strategies in the market.

How's your list of companies looking? Maybe you're beginning to narrow down your options. Or perhaps you have a few financial statements and stock charts to review first. Take your time—moving at your own pace is crucial in this journey. The stock market will always be there.

## FUND YOUR BROKERAGE ACCOUNT: WHERE THERE IS RISK, THERE IS OPPORTUNITY

Now that you know how the market works, how it reflects the economy and an individual company's performance, how to read a stock chart, and how to make wise choices about where you invest, it's time to fund your brokerage account. Go back to the budget you established in Step 4, the amount you decided you could afford to lose on a weekly or monthly basis, and move it into your brokerage account. This is your first deposit. Some of you may experience this as an easy and exciting moment, while others may hesitate and wonder if they should press the transfer button. If you are having doubts, explore their root cause and get to the bottom of the money wounds that are emerging from the depths of your subconscious so that you can begin to remove these emotional obstacles from your path. Be patient with yourself.

To get to the point where I could confidently hold my stocks and focus on my time horizon without freaking out about what was happening in the market, I first had to face that green-eyed monster that invades our psyche when dealing with money: greed. Remember that false belief we explored in Step 1, that wealthy people are greedy? Well, it's very likely it will come back to haunt you whenever you attempt to put money to work for you and use it to generate wealth. To fend it off, go to the arsenal of tools we have been collecting throughout these pages and make use of this Wealth Warrior Truth: *Wealth gives me options.* Repeat this truth like a mantra each time the feeling of greed tries to stop you from investing in yourself and your priorities. Remember: the desire to build wealth does not make you greedy; it makes you a forward thinker who is looking out for your future and those of the generations to come.

Once I safeguarded my fortress from the green monster by not making impulsive decisions based on fear, I still had to deal with the fearmongering voices in my head: *The stock market is for white people. You are not smart or white. You're going to lose it all. This is way too risky. Who do you think you are?* Those thoughts were directly related to my scarcity mindset, and it was time to shut them the hell up. We must remind ourselves that the dollar amount we have decided to invest is the amount that we have already determined we can afford to lose. It's money that will not affect our bottom line when it's no longer in our pockets. If you're still feeling insecure, take a breather. Remember: scared money don't make money.

New shots at growth will always come with risk. But where there is risk, there is opportunity. When we're emotionally attached to our money, it can sabotage our wealth journey. We tend to equate our money with our worth, but in order to build wealth, we have to be able to let money go. My initial commitment, the monthly amount I decided I could afford to lose, was $208. After my first year of investing came to a close and I saw Netflix's stock price jump from $13 to $52, I doubled down on my conviction, revisited my budget, calculated my frivolous expenses, and decided I could afford to invest $416 a month during my second year in the market. Although it was what I could afford to lose, I still found it jarring to let go of what amounted to a monthly car payment; however, I constantly reminded myself that I was an investor who was now experiencing ownership of an itsy-bitsy part of a company. Through forward thinking, I could sense that this was only the beginning of my stock market journey. Reevaluating my expenses and realizing that I had *more* I could put in the market reinforced my ability to feel less emotionally connected or dependent on that specific amount of money. I knew that, worst case, I could live without it; and best (and most likely) case, that money would come back to me two-, three-, or tenfold. Taking this risk was crucial in shifting my perspective and becoming more comfortable with my surroundings.

Now it's your turn. Go to your brokerage, and move the first installment of your established budget into your account.

I highly recommend setting up automatic deposits from here on out, as you have likely done with your high-yield savings account, streaming services, cell phone bill, or other bills or online subscriptions. It's a great way to emotionally detach from that money, because you won't have to manually transfer it every month and risk facing more doubts and fears that could stop you in your tracks.

---

### WEALTH WARRIOR TACTICS:
#### *TAKE YOUR TIME*

Funding your brokerage account doesn't mean you have to invest that money right away. It simply means you have transferred money into an account that will give you access to whatever stocks you're looking to purchase. Take your time. If you aren't considering fractional shares, you may even have to save up in your brokerage account to purchase a particular stock you want at its current price. Continue to do your homework and get a feel for the market and your potential investments as you enter this space. Don't feel like you have to know how to do the butterfly in the pool now that you've funded your account. You will drown, and I won't be able to save you. Hang out in the shallow end for a while, hold on to the ledge as long as you need to, doggy-paddle until you feel confident enough to swim into deeper waters.

## PICK ONE TO THREE STOCKS: LESS IS MORE

As the funds deposited into your brokerage clear—this can take a few days—go back to your list of potential companies, the ones you know and have now analyzed on a deeper level, and, armed with all this valuable info, start thinking about the one to three stocks you would like to officially invest in. Choosing only one to three will prevent you from spreading your monthly investment too thin. If you invest in one to three stocks, you'll be able to keep up with them through continued research and by tuning in to their quarterly earnings calls while learning how to become a diligent and responsible investor. Remember that this is not just a click-and-go situation. As Wealth Warriors, we are active learners when it comes to where and how our money is working for us.

The first few years in the market are all about training and solidifying your knowledge in this space. The time you put in to do so is also an investment in yourself. So if you are already squeezed for time, consider narrowing your list down to one stock just to get your feet wet. If you feel you can handle a little more, then go for two or three, but no more than that to start. Overdiversifying at such an early stage in your investing journey is a recipe for potential loss and tidal waves of anxiety. It's like trying to save for multiple goals at once versus focusing on one thing at a time. Being in the market for the first time will already be a roller coaster in itself. Imagine navigating that seesaw of emotions with a bunch of stocks you can't keep up with. Nope, not happening on my watch. With time in the market, your moves will eventually level up.

## WEALTH WARRIOR TACTICS:
### *AN ETF AIN'T A STOCK; IT'S A BASKET*

An **ETF** is an exchange-traded fund, a basket of stocks that trades similarly to individual stocks but is not limited to one sector. It's like one of those luxurious holiday baskets filled with chocolates, dried fruits, a mug, jams, crackers, and more. You can purchase an ETF the same way you purchase shares. I use ETFs to invest in specific areas that my research has led me to understand are the future but that I don't necessarily grasp well enough yet to make an informed decision regarding individual stocks. Some investors like the diversification an ETF provides. In this book, we are focusing on individual stocks and not ETFs, because I want you to learn how to be a direct owner in the market, picking out your own stocks, but it's important for you to be aware of what ETFs are in case they align with your intentions, of course. Remember: each wealth-building journey is different. Once you get the fundamentals straight, you will have the basic know-how to start discovering what path may work best for you.

I was a steadfast stock monogamist when I entered the market. From 2013 to 2018, the only stock I invested in was Netflix. At first, this strategy fit my comfort level. I was still in learning mode, and I didn't want to make any unnecessary waves. After my first year in the market, during which I watched the stock price start at $13, then jump to $23 after that quarter's earnings call, which was when I first bought shares, and later rise to $52 a share, I was elated by how my money had multiplied, so, as I mentioned earlier, I went ahead and doubled down on my established budget. I was so hyped, I couldn't wait to see the kind of money I would make in year two, but then... nothing happened.

At the start of 2014, the stock was around $50 a pop, and by the end of the year, after seeing lows of $42 and highs of $69, it remained at around $50 a share. I had invested $416 a month that year in hopes of seeing growth in my account, but other than my own investment, it remained stagnant, and many of my money wounds began to haunt me once again. Those damn wounds are funny like that. You may think you have them under control, but they come roaring back with the slightest trigger. I had to once again work on emotionally detaching from this money and remind myself that I wasn't in it to make a quick buck; I was in it for the long haul. I can't even begin to imagine having to deal with these emotions while holding more than a few stocks in my portfolio—that might've pushed me to the edge and made me back out. But I stayed the course and committed to not selling any of my shares. My perspective and outlook on the business I was investing in began to grow. I was now looking at things from a business's and an investor's perspective. Meetings with our CEO suddenly mattered to me. Soon, investing became more than just the automatic deposit going from my checking account to my brokerage account each month. I was an active participant in my wealth-generating journey—fueled by knowledge, good planning, and a hunger to reach my financial goals. I also began trusting myself and my decisions more while witnessing my relationship with money ease and evolve, because now I wasn't just saving desperately to survive; I was putting money to work for me.

And then I got scared.

I continued to invest the same $416 per month into Netflix stock in year three of my wealth-building journey, but I didn't dare add another stock to my portfolio. At one point, I identified an opportunity with Adidas right before it launched its very first collaboration with Kanye West for the Adidas Yeezy, which I knew would be a huge deal. Adidas at the time was trading at $30 a share. I had a serious conversation with my partner, Alfonso, about buying some of this stock, but then fear possessed my rationale and I was toast. *What if we lose it all?* I asked myself. Despite the fact that I'd been in the market for two full years, it all still felt pretty new and overwhelming to me, so I backed down and let fear win that day. When the Yeezy line was launched, we watched from the sidelines as Adidas stock soared up 400 percent within the next several years. And that became my pattern for the following three years. I stood by and simply observed other stocks and did a shit ton of research yet didn't dare to venture into new territory. In retrospect, if I'd had someone guiding me through these steps and encouraging me to make bold yet carefully researched money moves while assessing my emotions along the way, I wouldn't have waited until 2018 to pick another stock. As you narrow down your choices to one to three publicly traded companies, let's look at another important factor to consider before you enter this territory.

## CREATE AN EXIT PLAN

You have to be persistent, stay the course, be in it for the long haul, but there are times when you will need to hit the road and sell an investment before meeting your long-term horizon. That's why I advise you to create an exit plan ahead of buying a stock and understand the many variables at play that must be considered before enacting it and pressing that sell button—it really will vary on a case-by-case basis, but here are some general red flags to keep in mind. Market shifts can happen overnight, and you have to be prepared to move swiftly if they do. Your exit plan is a list of markers that you need to pay attention to that will help inform you if the time has come to get out.

Four big markers to keep your eyes peeled for are if the company changes direction from its existing business model; if it's acquired by another company—like when Elon Musk bought Twitter and expressed he would be taking the company private; if there's a chance another company may disrupt the product you're invested in and the prospect is beginning to affect its earnings—like Netflix's impact on Blockbuster; or if the CEO steps down. Keep in mind that just because a CEO steps down doesn't mean you immediately have to sell out of your position. When Jeff Bezos stepped down as CEO of Amazon, he already had a groomed, experienced candidate waiting in the wings, making the transition quite seamless. A red flag in this case would be if there is no clear successor or if that person has no training or experience in this area. If that's the case, do some more digging and see if this is reason enough to exit this investment.

When one or more of these markers appear on your radar, they may affect your conviction in the investment, that is, why you believed in the company to begin with. If your conviction has clearly pivoted given the new turn of events, then it may be time to consider selling. Think of these markers as the Lego pieces in a fully constructed set that represents our conviction. So, when the CEO of a company leaves and we don't believe their successor is ready to take on this position, we don't necessarily dismantle our entire Lego construction, we simply remove that piece. The construction may teeter a little, but it will likely remain standing. Now, if we start removing more pieces due to other red-flag markers, then our conviction may become wobblier. You want to aim to exit before the entire construction caves in.

These exit plan decisions will be based on your research and also on your money intentions. Your current intention is to simply step into the market with a small budget, purchasing only one to three carefully chosen stocks that will hopefully not require you to enact any exit plan in the short term. Now, to be clear, I'm not suggesting you have to stay in a stock for the rest of your life either. Once you have reached your long-term goal and made enough money, say, for a down payment on your future house (that's how I used some of my Netflix stock!)—or if you've identified a better investment opportunity with more growth, then that too may be a signal indicating you are ready to move on. You will fine-tune these strategies as you become a seasoned investor.

## BUY IN: YOUR FIRST SHARE IS ALREADY AN ASSET

Okay, so you now know all about the market, you're clear on how to analyze a company using its financial statements and quarterly earnings calls, you've done your research to back your conviction, you've funded your account, and you have an exit plan—this is it. It's time to purchase your first shares!

Go to your brokerage account, add how many shares you want to buy from your chosen stock, then click the buy button. Ta-da: you are officially a shareholder! You have an asset. Now the real work begins. You must exercise patience as you watch your money move in the market. You will witness losses and you will witness gains. Your money wounds will come back in full force, but before you know it, you'll notice healthier patterns of thought and decision-making, so long as you stay committed to excavating and truly addressing that baggage. It may sound scary now, but it's so exciting! Invest in what you know: choose the stocks that will give you the most peace and allow you to sleep at night. Money has kept us up for way too long—get that money and rest easy!

# MONEY IS NOW WORKING FOR YOU: DON'T FORGET TO ASK FOR EXTRA PICKLES

El dinero me llueve, diablo qué aguacero, en la cuenta
un par de ceros, y empezamos desde cero.*

—*Bad Bunny*

Is it hard for you to receive anything, such as gifts, compliments, or payment for your services? Now that you've begun to deploy money in the stock market, preparing to become a recipient is essential, and that means going head-to-head with your money wounds again. Shadows of your old belief system that may still

---

* Money rains, fuck, what a downpour, a couple of zeros in the account, and we started from zero.

be lurking in the dark will be revealed when you identify how you feel about your gains. This is how we continue shifting from a toxic relationship with money to a healthy wealth mindset in which we no longer have to carry the weight of our generational wounds and can finally see money for what it is: a tool to improve our lives.

Oftentimes we don't even realize the shame we carry or the feeling of unworthiness that haunts our decisions until the roles are reversed, and we go from giving all we've got to actually receiving compensation for our efforts. We've learned how to wave that moment off instead of accepting it as something we deserve. That's why in order to prepare to become a recipient in the stock market, we first must take an honest look at our behavior with money out in the real world.

## PREPARE TO BECOME A RECIPIENT

It was July 2015. I was nearing my third year investing in the stock market. After weathering the previous year, when my shares had started and ended at around fifty dollars, I was in it to win it, and ready to stick it out for the next seven years of my time horizon. All was evolving well on that front, but at Netflix I was miserable. Overworked doesn't even begin to cover it. That year, I had discovered that while I was busting my ass retrieving seventeen thousand assets (TV shows and movies and all things attached to them, from dubs to subtitles) from Latin America, some of my colleagues were moving only three hundred to four hundred assets. My jaw dropped to the basement. There I was, heart in my throat on the daily knowing I had to hit certain deadlines, without having taken a vacation in twenty-four months, while other employees were handling a fraction of a fraction of my workload. I was at a breaking point, so I vocalized this newfound knowledge to my manager and decided to take a much-deserved vacation. As toxic as this environment had become in my life, I feared quitting. In my eyes, leaving a job that I'd toiled to get and toiled to keep would mean not just losing my reputation for working at a top-notch, forward-thinking tech company, but also saying goodbye to the stability of having a salary. My money wounds around security and safety were steering my career path, and at the time I thought I had to buck up and deal with the situation.

After a few days off, which I used to realign myself with my needs and goals, I returned to the office and was called into a meeting with a manager whom I had never worked with directly, who told me I no longer fit the team's direction. I stared back at him stunned. Almost three years of carrying the bulk of the content for the team and, in what felt like a matter of minutes, I was escorted to my desk to gather my belongings and out to the street. And just like that, all my money-wound-driven fears fully manifested themselves.

That night I got home, broke the news to Alfonso, and spent the next several days crying into my pillow. I felt humiliated and devastated. I slowly began to realize how much of my identity had been tied to this job. Who would I be without the prestige that came with working at this coveted tech entertainment industry giant? What could I claim at industry events and Hollywood movie premieres other than my heavily bruised ego? Two weeks after my job at Netflix ended, after lying in bed writing in my tear-stained journal, attempting to sort through my emotions and identify my next move, when I began to come up for air, Alfonso called me from work.

"You're not going to believe what happened."

My heart dropped and I replied, "You got laid off."

"Yeah, the whole team got laid off. They're cleaning house."

A switch flipped within me, and I went from licking my wounds from my own layoff to jumping into Wealth Warrior action. I was technically still employed until the end of the month, so I used that as leverage to immediately refinance my car, which dropped my monthly payment substantially. And Alfonso and I made all the possible money moves at our disposal to cut back on our overhead. Two weeks later, I found out I was pregnant. I took in a deep breath and released it slowly to calm my nerves, yet I was also elated with the news. We had been trying since February of that year but never imagined it would happen in the thick of such unforeseen circumstances.

A week before I got laid off, my sister had approached me with the idea of us moving into the guest room of the three-bedroom house she shared with her husband in the South Bay region of Los Angeles. They were looking to grow their savings, and she knew we were actively saving up to one day buy a house. At the time, I politely declined, but given this new turn of events and that our lease for our one-bedroom apartment was up at the end of September, I felt this offer to be almost serendipitous.

"Look, I think we need to take my sister up on her offer," I said to Alfonso.

With a baby on the way, it was a no-brainer. So we packed all our belongings, stored most of our boxes in my sister's garage, and made our new home in her guest bedroom. It was an incredibly humbling experience, yet being with family during such a difficult transition filled me with great comfort. I felt extremely supported at a time when I should've been losing my shit.

We were surrounded by family, and I had received a severance check that would hold us over for close to a year, but the stress of our circumstances felt like a block of cement on my chest. I started having flashbacks to when I was pregnant at thirteen with my daughter. The circumstances were similar: I faced major instability, moved out of one house and into another, and generally felt helpless and clueless about what the future might hold for me and my baby. *How could this be happening to me again, more than twenty years later?* I was freaking thirty-five years old, an age when you're supposed to start reaping the rewards of your hard work. I was supposed to have a home in my name to show for it. I was supposed to have a steady job. I was supposed to approach this planned pregnancy with a calm and joyous state of mind. As these thoughts swarmed my mind, Alfonso fell into a deep depression of his own. Months went by with no job prospects in sight for either of us; we were blowing through my severance, dipping into our opportunity fund to survive. And instead of proudly displaying my growing belly, I had to hide it each time I walked into an interview so as to not be rejected because of this new life developing within me. I exited each meeting hoping to get the "You're hired" call and dreading having to accept a job and later say, "By the way, I'm pregnant." This was not how it was all supposed to go.

I might not have known how we were going to get out of this hole we'd been plunged into, but selling my stock was not an option. Not even these extenuating circumstances swayed my conviction. When the mere idea crept into my mind, I clung to Reed Hastings's statement: "It's not about what's happening today; it's about what will happen twenty years from now." I watched some of my colleagues get laid off and sell their shares out of spite or anger. I'm not going to lie; my bubbling fury felt like a volcano on the verge of erupting, but I had done enough research to see beyond this moment and continue to bank on the vision of Reed Hastings. I had faith that trusting the process would eventually turn my money into something bountiful.

If there is one thing we are guaranteed in life, it's that there are no guarantees. We will all face similar moments in our wealth-building journey that will test our conviction in our stock choices and in the market. But if we do our due diligence, remain focused on our money intentions, and are ready to become recipients, we will also have the power to realize that the stock market is one of the few places where our money can work for us while we get back on track. Now more than ever I needed my investment to grow so we could buy the house I had envisioned when I first entered the stock market. My commitment to my shares, my long-term time horizon, and my exit plan—to not selling out for anything other than major red-flag markers or to fulfill my intention of homeownership—became a source of stability that I used to push myself to become more resourceful and find other ways to bring in income.

A year after we moved in with my sister, Alfonso and I took an "if we build it, they will come" leap of faith. The last thing I wanted to do was strain my relationship with my sister by overstaying our welcome. I told Alfonso that we couldn't keep waiting for these jobs to appear—we had to step out in faith and forge ahead. So we went from the confines of my sister's small guest bedroom, where we could barely fit a full-size bed, our then six-month-old son's bassinet, and a changing table, to a rental house in South Los Angeles. Three days after moving into our new home, Alfonso got hired for a full-time position. And soon after that, I landed a part-time contracting gig at Lionsgate, as part of the launch team for its new LA-based Spanish-language streaming service, Pantaya.

Meanwhile, I had already begun my path as a content creator. While pregnant with Benicio, I had started a YouTube channel filled with mommy content, including pregnancy, lifestyle, and mommy hacks. And in 2017 *Let There Be Luz*, the podcast that would become the pinnacle for change in my professional life, was born.

While recording those episodes, I really began to come face-to-face with my money wounds. Alfonso and I were still living paycheck to paycheck, barely making ends meet, and quickly being priced out of the house we were renting due to exorbitant yearly hikes. Meanwhile, Benicio was fast approaching school age, but I wasn't too keen on him entering our neighborhood's school system. Something had to give, yet anytime I thought about monetizing *Let There Be Luz*, I was overwhelmed with a sense of shame. I was getting used to seeing my money grow in the stock market and exercising patience and discipline in that area, but charging listeners for my spiritual content, even though it was gaining traction and I needed to generate more money, felt wrong. I couldn't marry the idea of money and spiritual content in my mind, so I didn't, until a happy accident forced me to open my eyes.

It was 2018 and I was about fifty episodes into my podcast when one morning, my son accidentally spilled water on my laptop, rendering it useless. With my listeners clamoring for more episodes and our tight budget at home, I wasn't sure how to move forward. As you can imagine, if I had not dipped into my stock during that dire period in 2015 when my partner and I were both jobless and awaiting the birth of our child, I sure as hell wasn't about to do it now. That money intention was still set on a future house for the three of us, so I stayed true to my conviction. And that inspired me to shift my mindset. While talking to a friend, I said, "What if I crowdfund to pay for my new laptop?"

"Nah, you can't do that. White people do that. You can't beg for money," was my friend's knee-jerk reaction.

Nowadays, people of color have tapped into crowdfunding (though we typically see less money headed our way than white people do, which is another battle still to be waged), but back in 2015 crowdfunding among my community for a passion project was pretty rare, especially for something like a laptop.

"But wait," I insisted. "Am I begging for money if I'm providing a podcast and they're hounding me for the next episode?"

I thought about this conversation for a minute. I had created an entire podcast without ever getting paid. Not one major sponsor backed me with money. The episodes, which I wrote and took up to eight hours to edit, were released every single week for free. And I had thousands of listeners enjoying my work. If they were so adamant about getting more content, surely they could make a onetime contribution. *I'm providing a service*, I said to myself, *and if there's a large enough group that wants my podcast to continue, then our community needs to begin to get comfortable with crowdfunding.* And I had to get comfortable with receiving. Nevertheless, a rush of guilt and unworthiness washed over me for thinking this way. I was upset because I felt I just didn't have what it took to create content full-time and successfully monetize it. I also had this nagging thought that kept coming up each time I tried to talk myself into being okay with this move: *How dare I demand help from the very people I am trying to help with my content?* I felt like I should be distributing laptops, not asking for help to get a new one.

As my thoughts and beliefs battled it out in my mind, I received a DM on Instagram from one of my podcast listeners who'd seen my recent posts about my circumstances. She offered me a hundred dollars for the laptop and added, "I think you should start a GoFundMe campaign." That was the sign I needed. It gave me the courage to trust my instinct, so I set up a campaign online and in less than twenty-four hours I had raised enough to replace my laptop.

This was a before-and-after moment in my life. I felt so much shame about having to crowdfund, yet my listeners felt no shame in demanding my free content, which they clearly found valuable. The shame that comes from the idea of crowdfunding in our community is the same shame we carry when we need to ask for help in other areas of our lives. But everyone needs support.

After I got the laptop, it wasn't all well and good with my online community. Some had an issue with my crowdfunding decision once they found out I owned shares in the stock market—and they called me out on it. Explaining my circumstances only helped cement my stance. Up until then, I had been giving away my content for free. This experience didn't just highlight my need to be assertive when it came to valuing the work I produced. It showed me I also had to be okay with becoming a recipient of abundance.

And that's what I want for you too. Now that you're beginning to invest in the stock market, with time, you will become a recipient, and you have to be ready for that moment. We must move on from our toxic relationship with money to a healthy wealth mindset that will prepare us to receive with an open mind and heart, because we are worthy of that and so much more. You deserve what you want to achieve—don't let anyone tell you otherwise. When I cut through our community's haggling mentality, understood my worth, and found myself on the other side of all my sacrifice and work, there was no turning back. Value yourself enough to invest and generate the wealth you deserve.

This lesson really hit home for me around three years later, when Alfonso, my son, Benicio, and I were smack in the middle of our big move from our rented apartment in Dallas—we'd moved to Texas from Los Angeles a year earlier—to a newly built house that we'd purchased, our very first home of our own. We hadn't eaten all day, so we stopped at the nearest McDonald's, where I ordered a cheap cheeseburger. As I wolfed it down, I thought, *This would be ten times better if it had more pickles.* The next day, I drove to McDonald's again and ordered the same cheese-burger, then paused for a fleeting second. *Should I ask for more pickles?* I wondered. It wouldn't have been an inconvenience, just an extra charge, and I could afford it now as my business was booming, but I said nothing. I paid, returned to my car, and as I sat there and sank my teeth into my burger, I felt the crunch I had dreamed about the previous day. In disbelief, I lifted the top bun and found a mountain of pickles fusing with the melted cheese, and I burst into happy tears. Those pickles symbolized what can happen when we open ourselves up to abundance in all areas of our lives, including in the stock market.

## GET TO KNOW YOUR PICKLES IN THE STOCK MARKET: GAINS AND LOSSES

The first time you receive extra pickles can be absolutely exhilarat-ing. You are worthy of those extra pickles, which in this case means you are worthy of receiving the capital gains you will make from your investments. Let's get into the deep core of what capital gains are exactly so you are prepared to openly receive these pickles.

Your initial investment in the stock market—that is, the money you use to purchase shares—is considered capital. Capital gains are the profit you make from that initial investment. And a loss happens when the initial value of your stock decreases in price. There are two types of capital gains and losses: unrealized and realized.

### Unrealized Gains and Losses

**Unrealized gains and losses**, also called paper gains and losses, are basically when the value of your shares increases or decreases in the stock market. Let's say you purchased one share of Apple stock valued at $100. You've decided to keep this share for five or more years because you're all about that long-term horizon. As time passes and you watch that share in the market, you will see its value go up and down. So if in nine months it is at $130, that means in that moment you have an unrealized gain of $30. And if in another nine months it's at $95, then you have an unrealized loss of $5. The market, as you now know, will continuously fluctuate, but you cannot lose more than your buy-in price of $100 (which is what you decided you could afford to lose in the first place). The upside is that there are no restrictions on what you can gain, so with time, you could potentially earn an unlimited amount of money from your initial $100 investment.

Unrealized gains and losses live in your brokerage account and are not taxed, because they are not real yet. As the years went by, while we struggled to get back on our feet, I saw the value in my Netflix stock rise, but I exercised discipline and didn't touch those gains, so they remained unrealized. To make them real, I would have had to sell out of my position. When we do that, then those gains or losses become *realized*.

*Realized Gains and Losses*

Selling your shares is the act of realizing your gains or your losses. **Realized gains and losses** are the difference between the original cost of a share and the current market value of that share at the time it is sold. Let's go back to our $100 Apple share. You're in it to win it for the long haul, but shit happens. Imagine that five months after your initial purchase, Apple's CEO decides to up and quit, the company decides to take a completely different direction, and the stock price drops to $75. Without this person at the helm of the company, you no longer have the same conviction in this investment, so you decide to implement your exit plan and sell your share. In that moment, you realize a loss of $25. This is now real as in realized, which in Wall Street speak means you took the loss.

Now, imagine that the CEO's exit doesn't shake your conviction in the company. Its earnings calls and sales have reinforced your belief in this company, so you decide not to sell and instead stick to your long-term horizon. Five years go by, and the stock is now at $300. The $200 in unrealized growth and positive earnings calls help strengthen your conviction. At this point, I would hope that this would inspire you to increase your time horizon from five to ten years and continue to play chess, not checkers, in the market, like Warren Buffett and his thirty-plus years holding Coke stock. But for the sake of this example, let's say you decide to sell because this $200 gain fulfills your original money intention. In that moment, those extra $200 become a realized gain.

When I reached the amount I needed for a down payment on a house with my Netflix stock, I decided to sell a third of my shares and use those gains to fulfill my money intention. I never lifted a finger for these gains. These were my crunchy, juicy extra pickles in the market that I openly received after putting my money into a stock I had conviction in and then exercising unrelenting patience and discipline to stick with my long-term time horizon and not sell out too soon.

---

### WEALTH WARRIOR TACTICS:
### *WHAT TO DO WITH THE EXTRA PICKLES CALLED DIVIDENDS*

If you've invested in a dividend stock, your extra pickles may also come in the form of dividends—that is, the money corporations decide to give to their shareholders as a reward for investing in their companies. Dividends are paid in cash, and even if the stock is down, they will usually land in your brokerage account on a quarterly basis but could also be distributed monthly, semiannually, or annually, depending on the corporation's preferences. They usually consist of a few cents or dollars, so rather than withdrawing these extra pickles, I've got one word for you: reinvest. Either automatically reinvest them in the stock (check with your brokerage firm—there's usually a box you can check to make this happen) or combine these extra pickles with your monthly investment budget and use them to continue building your position in the one to three stocks of your choice.

---

## GET DOWN TO THE NITTY-GRITTY
## WITH YOUR TAXES

I have often heard people in our community say that they refuse to invest in the stock market because they're afraid of having to pay more taxes. I get it. This is a totally normal feeling, especially in our communities of color, but it must be addressed. I had to work through that same fear myself. It's linked to our scarcity mentality, the one that pushes us to cling to every last cent. But it's time to shift our perspective. *Taxes* should not be a word that incites fear. Think about it: Do you say to yourself, *I'm not going to work, because I don't want to pay taxes*? Do you think, *Oh, I hope I don't get that promotion or raise, because that will push me into another income tax bracket*? No. You go to work. You climb that ladder. You get that high-paying position, promotion, or raise. You don't let the thought of taxes stop you from aiming high in your career. So that shouldn't stop you from investing and participating in this wealth-building arena either.

When you sell your shares and realize your gains, there will be taxes to be paid—that's a fact. But remember the lesson from the financial statements section we covered in the previous chapter: it takes money to make money. That's not a bad thing. I'll break down some of the basics next, but remember: the key to this part of your journey is to have a kick-ass CPA who can teach you tax-saving techniques and strategies that are tailored to your needs. So take the following info as an overview, and then go talk to your CPA about how to move forward.

First and foremost, you will be taxed only on your realized gains (profit), not your initial investment. In other words, if you bought a share at $100 and sold it for $150, you will be taxed only on the $50 gain on your initial investment of $100, not the full $150. Let's say you have to pay 15 percent tax on the $50—that means $7.50 will go to taxes (make sure to set this amount aside so that when tax day rolls around, it doesn't catch you by surprise) and the remaining $42.50 will go into your pocket. In other words, your capital gain itself will cover the taxes you owe—again, stash that percentage away so you don't accidentally spend it before income taxes are due.

Keep in mind that the amount of tax you pay on your gains will also depend on how long you held those assets before cashing out. If you buy a share and sell it in less than a year, that will fall under the short-term capital gains tax, which is usually the same rate as your income tax bracket. Now, if you hold that same share for more than a year, it will fall under the long-term capital gains tax, which as of writing this section has rates of 0 percent, 15 percent, or 20 percent, depending on your taxable income and filing status. In a nutshell, the tax for long-term capital gains is usually lower than the one for short-term capital gains—yet another reason to stick to your long-term horizon. As you can see, there are some moving pieces depending on your particular status, so checking in with your CPA to determine your rate in the short and long term is crucial.

One last note: throughout the year, when you sell a share, you won't pay income tax at that specific moment. You will be taxed for the total shares you have sold and the gains or losses you have realized at the end of the year. That's when your brokerage will produce a form known as a 1099 to report your gains and losses to the IRS, which will also be made accessible to you. During tax season, once you receive notice that this form is available for downloading (or once you receive it in the mail), you should take it to your CPA for them to account for any assets sold and calculate the income taxes due. If you sell out of shares and there's a loss instead of a gain, that loss can be deducted against your realized capital gains. A realized loss can also offset your regular income up to a certain amount—another reason to first and foremost consult with your CPA. Now, if you did not sell any shares during the year, then you will not receive a 1099, nothing will be reported to the IRS, and you will not need to take any further action on those unrealized gains or losses. Reporting happens only on realized gains and losses when shares are sold.

## OWN YOUR WEALTH-BUILDING WARRIOR STATUS

When my money started to grow in my brokerage account, it was absolutely mind blowing. I realized it was the easiest way to generate money. I didn't have to endure a demanding boss or endless work hours for a fixed paycheck. I just had to do my due diligence, choose solid companies, and put that money in there so that it could now work for me. I had never experienced anything like that before.

A big part of this journey, once you've learned the basic steps of how to get started, is realizing how to get smarter and savvier within this space. When you understand money and utilize it as it was intended, it will generate a level of freedom those in power don't want people of color, immigrants, or their children to have. To lay the foundation to build our wealth, we have to break free from and reframe our impoverished perspective, and learn to ask for and receive more. Nowadays, I never order a burger without asking for extra pickles, and neither should you.

# STEP 7

# BUILD YOUR WEALTH: ALLOW YOURSELF TO IMAGINE MORE

> Stay far from timid, only make moves when your heart's in it, and live the phrase "Sky's the limit."
>
> —*Biggie Smalls, a.k.a. the Notorious B.I.G.*

When you first enter the stock market, it will feel like a thrill ride. Owning your carefully chosen stock will likely make your chest swell with pride. Exhilaration over breaking barriers and occupying this new space like the Wealth Warrior that you are will have you fueled up and ready to climb Mount Everest. You're there, you're putting your knowledge and money to work for you, and you're revved up for whatever comes next. Bring it on! But what comes after purchasing your one to three stocks and finally getting used to how the market breathes will likely be...pretty boring. But boring is good. Boring means you're not overdiversifying and spreading yourself too thin. Boring means you're probably feeling more comfortable in this space after navigating the learning curve that is the first year in the market. And this, in turn, may indicate that you are ready to double down on the quintessential intention behind making this money: building generational wealth.

## STOCK YOUR PANTRY

New investors often get caught up in the whirlwind of excitement and start buying one share of this, another share of that, and then suddenly they may have bought into forty different companies but have only one share of each. Now that you have your one to three stocks, don't get distracted by the latest bright and shiny company to take over the finance headlines—stick to your guns and keep building your current positions. Imagine your portfolio is a pantry. The objective of a pantry is to hold goods that are meant to last one, two, three weeks or even months down the line. With enough of your key ingredients, you will eventually be able to serve your family a feast. But that can't happen with a couple of frijoles, a few grains of rice, a quarter of a tortilla, and a teaspoon of salsa. If you overdiversify by investing in everything to a very small degree, it's almost like you're investing in nothing.

So, let's say you currently own two stocks: one canister of frijoles and one canister of rice. (I know, how can we live without salsa? But patience, Warrior—that will come later.) How many frijoles do you currently have in that canister? You know damn well that three frijolitos will not even make you a taco, let alone enough for your entire family. What about your canister of rice? You'll need more than five grains of rice to make a feast, right? So you need to focus on filling these two canisters first, using your allotted budget to slowly build your positions—that is, the shares you've purchased—with your two chosen companies, before you move on to the next canister in your pantry. Remember: the objective of your portfolio is to provide a building block toward something greater for you and your family in the future. By staying the course and adding to each canister slowly but surely, you'll not only grow your shares but likely lower your **cost basis** (the average value of all the shares you own).

Let's go back to the Apple stock example for a beat. Say you bought three shares of Apple. The first one was $100. The second one was $150. And the third was $50. If you add these three shares and divide them by three, you will get your cost basis, which would be $100. If the stock goes down and your budget allows it, you can buy shares at a lower price, which in stock market slang is known as "buying the dip," and lower your cost basis average. This means that when the stock is once again increasing in price, you will eventually hit your break-even point—the average dollar amount with which you bought these shares—and enter positive territory sooner. I get a thrill out of doing this.

Focusing on long-term investing will very likely lead to capital growth. First, you'll notice you have enough to make yourself a plate of rice and beans, awesome! But don't stop there. The intention is to build generational wealth, so you want to be able to make una olla de frijoles con arroz to serve that feast you envisioned when you first entered the market. With time, the magical pantry that is the stock market will grow your pantry stash, and one day you'll wake up to a full canister of frijoles and another one of rice. That's when you can start considering deploying your allotted budget to add salsa to your pantry to serve at the feast.

You can't eat arroz con frijoles forever, though, right? So when do you buy the tortillas and the salsa? When you have enough frijoles and rice to serve a feast. In other words, when you start hitting your money intentions. I held Netflix stock for seven years before I bought a new stock. I didn't have a job for a while, so I wasn't in a position to deploy more cash into the stock market. As I let my current investment grow, I focused my efforts away from investing more money (money that I now could *not* afford to lose) and invested my time in more research. Holding your shares without buying or selling is also a strong position in the market. I wanted to be ready for when I was no longer living paycheck to paycheck, and let me tell you, those years were incredibly educational. Holding my position in Netflix while navigating the stock market and remaining a student in this space made me feel mature and fortified my confidence as an investor. There was no erratic teenage energy in my decision-making. I was being driven not by impulses but rather by research. The ability to understand that money is a tool and I need that tool to survive day in and day out—from turning on a light at home and driving to even taking a walk in our local park (its maintenance is paid for by our local taxes)—enabled me to tackle my false beliefs and fortify my mindset in all areas of my life.

This journey is like learning how to ride a bike. During your first few years in the stock market, you will have your training wheels on to support you when you feel wobbly. With time and experience, you will grow more confident, and just like when you learn how to ride a bike, you'll know when you feel steady enough to take the training wheels off and continue your journey on two wheels. You'll notice this maturity and growth as an investor when you begin to read financial statements and check stock price levels with ease, when you listen to the latest financial headlines and know how that information may or may not affect your stocks, and when you see a slump in the stock market as an opportunity to buy in and lower your cost basis instead of hyperventilating and entering panic mode. This will all signal that it may be time to add a new ingredient to your pantry. If you feel you've reached that point, then ask yourself, *Are my current holdings well stocked? Do I have the time to carefully research another stock? Do I have the time to fit in an extra hour to read financial statements and listen to earnings calls each quarter?* If the answer is yes, then you may be ready to add another ingredient to your pantry. That's the way to do it.

**WEALTH WARRIOR TACTICS:**
*REASSESS YOUR BUDGET*

Once you become more comfortable in the stock market, revisit your budget and see if you can afford to bump it up a notch. If you feel you can handle adding an extra ten dollars a month to your investments, give it a shot. If after a month or two this bump feels overwhelming, readjust back to the original sum you decided you could comfortably afford to lose. The amount you can contribute per month or year will depend on your life circumstances. If shit hits the fan and money becomes tight, you may have to hold off on your monthly contributions altogether until things stabilize, and that's okay too. Take care of yourself, and as soon as you hit your stride again, revisit your budget and ramp it back up. Then continue to check in every three to six months to reassess the money you can afford to lose, and adjust as needed.

## FORTIFY YOUR WEALTH WARRIOR MINDSET

The fear during the dreaded red days, the euphoria of the green ones, and the anxiety that comes with investing in the stock market in general can all be exhausting. Allowing yourself to move through this process slowly and fully aware of each step you are taking will help build your investing muscle. I know talking about emotions yet again may sound redundant, but money wounds are redundant. For many of us, it's likely that we've been in scarcity mode longer than we've been in wealth-building mode. The false beliefs that we picked up are persistent, exhausting, and something we will consistently have to push up against as we climb to new financial heights and experience unfamiliar challenges.

The market brought my money wounds and emotions right up in my face. There was no looking away. Sure, there were rules to follow—find a company, buy the shares, and hold them—but I had to relinquish control to the market's breathing process. I had to push myself to practice discipline when my fears were screaming at me to sell everything and run for the hills before it was too late. I had to face my false beliefs and those voices in my mind speaking for my money wounds and learn how to shut them down with the knowledge I was gaining in the market. I had to deal with them to move forward and so do you, so let's shift our energy in that direction once more and dig in together. I want you to learn how to identify the emotions that will creep up on you while you're in the market, so you can take control, steady yourself, and have the discernment to make winning decisions.

### Fear Ain't Got Nothing on You

As I mentioned earlier, the market always bounces back, but that doesn't mean we shouldn't be prepared to deal with how we feel when it's falling. Brushing emotions under the rug is not the Wealth Warrior way. We have to understand and process our emotions through the good, the bad, and the ugly to come out triumphant on the other side. The truth is that the market does not like uncertainty—who does, right?—and when it senses no clear economic road map moving forward at a national and international level, it can become very volatile. When the stock market becomes volatile, it can feel like all bets are off for us. The big clickbaity headlines scare us into believing we should sell out before it's too late or buy in before we miss the opportunity of a lifetime, and this causes stocks to rise or fall dramatically. It's like all the patience and discipline and control we've been diligently exercising magically float out the window and we're suddenly standing in the middle of an open field and our enemies—stress, anxiety, and fear—are coming at us from all directions.

The thing is, fear can be an overriding emotion we may experience when we deploy our money into the stock market: fear of buying in, fear of selling, fear of missing out. Yet there is something unique that takes place when we're cognizant of our fear and invest anyway. I learned early on that all my desires were waiting for me as soon as I crossed the threshold of my fear. That's actually been my internal compass since I was a kid. When I was scared of the dark, I set out to face my fear and crawled under my bed to explore what was keeping me up at night. And that's the first time I realized that fear is a false narrative we create in our minds. So instead of cowering in a corner, I decided to learn from those times when I faced and conquered my fears. As the years passed and I entered the workforce, I spent years journaling and doing inner work to let go of scarcity-driven fear that came with not having enough money as a kid to buy toothpaste, shampoo, or underwear. And I managed to tackle it to the ground. But nothing taught me more about this emotion than the market.

I had my first freak-out when Disney announced its streaming service Disney+ in 2016, which they later officially launched in 2019. Netflix shares tumbled, and my heart jumped to my throat. Panic stricken, I kept staring at the screen and thinking, *Is it going to keep dropping?* Suddenly there was new competition on the block. Some of my friends quickly moved to sell their positions, but rather than follow their lead, I texted my money-conscious fam: "I think I'm going to sell out of Netflix."

"Tell us why," Bricia replied.

"Because Disney just announced they're planning to create a streaming service!"

Then Patty chimed in, "Keep Netflix and just buy Disney stock."

While I did not buy Disney stock, Patty's brilliant reply definitely made me stop and really think this through. She was right, multiple players could exist in this game. Her one-line text immediately pushed me from the scarcity mindset that was beginning to take control to one of great abundance. I was able to move past my panic-stricken mode and stand my ground. I understood this company; I knew and believed in its vision, so as terrifying as this short-term **volatility** was at times, I also realized it was just noise. I continued to commit to myself and my intentions while having compassion for myself. Three years later I was able to use a part of my gains, which continued to grow after this slight setback, to purchase my home.

I didn't let fear win, and neither should you. The act of sitting back and watching our stocks go up, come down, and then shoot up again will arm us with the power to know better when fear starts yelling at us to sell out before it's too late. This is all part of getting to know ourselves. Our reactions to the market will slowly reveal if we are risk-takers or risk averse. And this in turn will inform us of the stock or sector that suits us best. So embrace the emotions you feel as you navigate through this space. They will be some of your best teachers.

---

### WEALTH WARRIOR TACTICS:
### *HOW TO SURVIVE A MARKET CORRECTION*

As we discussed in Step 4, page 137, a correction is when the market pulls back more than 10 percent and less than 20 percent. We can expect to experience these at least once a year. As a new investor, this might be a little fear inducing when it happens to you for the first time; however, if you keep these tips in your back pocket and reach out for support to your money-conscious fam, you will be just fine!

✓ Stay calm and breathe.

✓ Ease up on checking the market on a daily basis if you're not buying.

✓ Don't obsess over your portfolio. It will be a roller coaster, but the ride will eventually end and balance will be restored.

✓ Find opportunities and buy the dip to lower your cost basis.

✓ Remember your long-term goal—think years and decades rather than days or weeks.

✓ Hold tight. Remember: you can't lose if you don't sell, and holding your shares is also a strong position.

## Tell Euphoria to Calm the Fuck Down

As scary as the market can feel as a new investor, it can also flip the switch on you and become the ultimate joy ride. If you've done your research and made a wise investment, your stock will likely start to go up. As people of color who are stepping into this space for the first time, we will see this abrupt rise as easy money, so to speak. You will suddenly feel like Wonder Woman discovering her superhuman speed for the first time. That sense of elation is called euphoria, and just as quickly as it sweeps you off your feet, it can take over and eventually land you flat on your ass. Euphoria has a way of making us feel we're invincible, smarter than the market, smarter than the experts, and that can spur us into making reckless, power-hungry decisions, like purchasing shares when we see a popular stock running up.

Right now, when I think of euphoria, I think of Tesla in 2020. After hesitating to buy in the previous year, I finally decided to take the plunge when the market crashed due to the pandemic. That stock proceeded to have massive swings with explosive growth in gains of up to a hundred dollars in a day that year, and I would be remiss to say that this roller-coaster ride didn't easily tickle my own euphoria. But I reminded myself that, like all other stocks, Tesla would not maintain a steady rise indefinitely—and it didn't; it was actually extremely volatile at the time. To remain levelheaded amid the excitement surrounding those fabulous green days, I looked at the charts to remind myself that the lines are not straight. There are peaks and valleys but rarely any plains. This helped me gather my emotions and find some much-needed balance.

I'm not going to lie; riding that wave when the market rallies is breathtaking, but what goes up must come down. Don't let euphoria get the best of you. When you feel that elation overpowering your senses, recall your money intentions, your long-term horizon, your research, and your rules so you can enjoy this high while not veering from your well-thought-out path.

## HIT THE ROAD: CUT YOUR LOSSES

Fear doesn't just have the power to keep us from investing; it can also push us to hold a position in the stock market for too long, and that can be equally detrimental to our wealth-building journey. When you see one of your stocks tank, how do you know if you should cut your losses or hold? My rule is to stay put in a stock and diligently follow the earnings calls. If I see the company no longer fits its vision or has already met its vision, then I may start considering enacting my exit plan to pull out. For example, going back to the stock I know like the back of my hand, I believe Netflix has reached its goal. It revolutionized streaming as we know it, has created original content outside of TV network standards, and has broken into the movie industry. Another reason I might consider selling stock is if there's a company I've diligently researched and I now feel even more excited about its prospects and vision than I do about the company I'm currently investing in. Then I may consider moving the money there. But sometimes shit doesn't go as planned. These are big lessons I had to learn the hard way.

It all began in 2020, at the height of the pandemic. We had recently moved to Texas, so I was mourning Los Angeles and questioning if this was the right decision for us, but Alfonso had landed a great job that would give me the chance to figure out my following steps. I had already pivoted into teaching about stocks, but I was still taking on big event-producing projects. I was also at a stalemate with my podcast, unsure of what type of content to produce going forward. *So, what's next?* I kept wondering. At the same time, we were good with money, I had a great portfolio in the market, and I felt safe. When stocks dropped, I knew this was an amazing opportunity to invest. I had been feeling solid about my choices so far until I made my first crucial mistake: I began to seek opportunities in sectors that I did not fully understand. I suddenly found myself dismissing my understanding of and established experience in the market and looking at what stock market tycoons like Warren Buffett and Charlie Munger were doing instead. I had emotional familiarity and experience with the tech sector and how it was disrupting the way we lived and shared information. I'd already learned to be okay with its volatility by being confident that growth would come in time. But oil businesses were something I did not understand and didn't really have a desire to learn about. Yet there I was, eyeing Nordic American Tanker (NAT), a company that stores oil in tankers.

I first heard of NAT from a well-known YouTuber who talks about the stocks he's investing in. I was intrigued by his conviction but not enough to start investing in the stock myself. Then I noticed other YouTubers making videos on the company too. I checked out the chart and thought, *It's only four dollars. Hmm, maybe I should consider buying this stock.* A few weeks later, I watched NAT's CEO forecast the incredible numbers the company would bring in for the next quarter's earnings on CNBC. His appearance on a major network made the opportunity feel more official. On the surface, it all seemed to make sense. The world was shutting down, so there was a significant decrease in the amount of oil we were using, because we were not driving, flying, cruising, manufacturing—we were all stuck at home. While our lives came to a screeching halt, oil production companies desperately needed a place to store the excess oil they were producing. Enter NAT. I sat with it for two days and then thought, *I can't let this opportunity go by!*

I thought this company would end up making a lot of money from its business during this time. The dollar signs flickered in my eyes, and greed blinded my judgment. Furthermore, instead of hitting pause and doing my own research, I made the mistake of leaning into other people's convictions and figured that would be enough. So I let greed take the wheel and made the impulsive (dare I say euphoric) decision to buy 338 shares at $7.79 a pop on April 28, 2020. I invested a total of $2,633.02 without even realizing that I was buying in during a really strong rally. FOMO at its finest. That was a shit ton of money for me to recklessly put into a stock that I barely understood. Heck, one dollar is a lot of money to put into a stock you don't get. But I convinced myself this was a good move. Given the info circling around the COVID-19 virus, I believed the pandemic would last through 2022, so I figured that would be a good time to sell out of this position, forgetting all about one of my original intentions: sticking to my long-term horizon to build generational wealth.

When investors buy into a stock because of FOMO and they do not understand the catalyst for what seems like a great opportunity, they are susceptible to what we call an organized pump and dump. A **pump and dump** is when a group of experienced traders organizes in chat communities like Reddit and Discord to purposely pump up a stock, creating buzz around it in the news, so that a ton of typically inexperienced investors will buy in quickly and drive the stock up. This pushes the stock to new all-time highs. That's when the experienced traders take immediate action and sell out—that is, dump the stock—multiplying their money, while the inexperienced investors who did not do their research are left on the losing side. Unfortunately, this happened to me. NAT's stock was hyped up by the YouTubers and the CEO's appearance on CNBC. That was the catalyst. Then, as the days rolled by, I started observing the stock completely break down, meaning there was a clear sell-off beginning to take place. The nail in the coffin was NAT's quarterly earnings call. Turned out the CEO had totally inflated the company's forecasted earnings on CNBC. My heart dropped. You'd think I would've jumped ship right then and there, but no, I clung to the mast of this sinking vessel in hopes that the stock would eventually move back up and I'd be able to at the very least sell out of my position and break even. In my opinion, when you start hoping for your stock to recover with no researched foundation—such as a clear path forward paved by the CEO—to back this hope, then you have likely lost all conviction in the company or, worse, as in my case, realized that you never had conviction in it to begin with. I started to play out my moves and reasoning in my head as I watched the stock tumble, and a crucial realization struck me: eventually the oil companies would slow down or stop pumping. That meant the need for oil storage was just a solution to a temporary problem. I. Fucked. Up. I needed to get out of this shit stat. And I had a chance.

After waiting for the stock to go up, desperately checking the chart every hour of every day, I saw a moment when the stock rallied, showing a slight sign of recovery. But instead of jumping on that opportunity and selling out, I got swept away by the hope that it would make its way closer to where I bought in, which tempered the fear of losing a big chunk of my capital and the sense of shame and embarrassment that came with it. That was the time to sell, when I began to come to terms with my mistake.

But I didn't cut my losses; I stayed. And its value dropped again. On July 6, 2020, I sold my 338 shares at $4.16 each, which equaled a total of $1,406.08. My cumulation of mistakes cost me $1,226.94 of my initial investment. Furthermore, I broke my stance as a long-term investor and made a short-term-trader move with a company I barely knew, going against all my rules. It just goes to show that even with seven years of experience, these emotions can still get the best of us if we're not careful.

Admitting we are wrong is never easy, especially when it comes to losing money. After years of exercising a deep sense of responsibility with money, I was drenched in shame from my reckless money move and didn't know how to bring myself to tell Alfonso what had happened. I had basically lost the equivalent of one month's rent at the time. I felt so guilty and irresponsible. How could I do this to my family? My shame quickly shifted into an ever-present anxiety that was eating away at me, and I knew the only way to nix it was to come clean. Alfonso has been by my side from the moment I embarked on my investment journey back in 2013. He's seen me study the market with a keen eye and carefully listen to earnings calls before deciding to invest in a stock. He's seen me take a leap and also freeze in fear. He's seen me meticulously comb through my mistakes and pull lessons from these moments. And all the while, he's made me feel supported, loved, and trusted. Alfonso knows that my mistakes are not in vain. And such was the case then too. He didn't get upset. He understood that this was part of my journey and there were bound to be hiccups along the way. His support as my partner and part of my money-conscious fam helped me breathe an enormous sigh of relief.

The industry calls these types of mistakes **market tuition**, which in a nutshell is the amount of money you lose as an investor in the stock market. It's the price we pay for the invaluable lessons we learn in the market, but that doesn't make such a loss any less painful. Nobody escapes market tuition, but very few dare talk about it, because of the shame these types of mistakes carry with them. What's more, by not knowing about market tuition, many new investors decide to retreat and quit after making such mistakes, thinking they're not cut out for this environment. But quitting is a mistake in and of itself. Allow yourself to be angry and pissed off about what didn't work out. Ask yourself what you could have done differently, what you did not see and why. Open yourself up to creative solutions, and turn these mistakes into new rules that will help safeguard you from making them again. Whatever your setback, know that it's happening for you and not to you—with money that you determined you could afford to lose. Then assess what your next move is going to be. If you feel you chose stocks without doing sufficient research and now your emotions—euphoria, greed, fear—are starting to make the decisions for you, then it may be time to revisit those companies and decide whether it's worth staying or cutting your losses and getting out—which is what I should've done earlier with NAT. Then deploy that money into another well-researched opportunity. Your mistakes should not make you quit the stock market altogether; they should strengthen you so that you can persevere with these newly acquired lessons. That's what makes you a Wealth Warrior.

After licking my wounds and digesting my lessons, I grabbed

the money I had left from this big mistake and purchased my first Tesla stock, following endless research and due diligence, of course. I moved back into the tech sector I know and love, with a stock I have a strong, long-term conviction in, and I have since made what I lost and more.

If you continue to situate yourself as a student in the market, remain disciplined in understanding this moneymaking machine, and accept your market tuition bill, you will not only get reimbursed for your losses but also start to see and comprehend the movement of money in ways you've never been exposed to before.

## DIVERSIFY BY REINVESTING

Your portfolio—that is, your grouping of financial assets, such as stocks, bonds, and cash—is your big-league fund. Not long ago, financial portfolios were mainly managed by finance professionals. But things have changed in the last decade or so, with big banks in the process of being decentralized by fintech and retail investors learning how to handle their own business. We now have the access to learn how to make our own mindful money moves, and I'm totally here for it.

I've made it clear that I don't believe in overdiversifying in the stock market. Stick with your one to three stocks, and when you're ready to add a couple more, continue to look to different sectors to maximize your returns and minimize risks. I made a misstep when I entered the oil industry with NAT, but that was just because I didn't do my due diligence, not because having stocks in different industries is a no-no. So don't be afraid of exploring industries and sectors other than the ones you currently participate in. Honestly, when I think of diversifying, I think of wealth-generating assets that go beyond the stock market. In other words, consider your stocks but also consider your retirement accounts, your opportunity fund, the real estate you own or may own one day, and all those wealth-generating investments we mentioned in Step 2, and set intentions to diversify in each of these areas. This will create different avenues of potential income that will bring great relief if you ever hit a snag or an emergency along your way. The goal is to build out your Monopoly board.

After five years of being invested only in Netflix, when both Alfonso and I once again had a steady stream of income, I decided to take the plunge and invest in a second stock. I felt so much empowerment from being the owner of one stock and being a longtime student of the stock market that I knew it was time for me to graduate and embody being an investor with a growing portfolio to show for it. It was important for me to step into that space and feel that for myself. So I started doing my research on a second stock and then another one that I was considering. I needed to get my bearings first, so I didn't jump into it immediately. And then 2020 happened.

I had been lying in wait for a crisis that would crash the market ever since I began this investment journey. Back in 2018, I kept reading and hearing experts say, "Every ten years there's a market crash. We're due for one at any moment." I had all my gear on and was ready to strike when the opportunity presented itself. That opportunity began to send signals in January 2020, when COVID-19 was already spreading in China. Then the pandemic hit our shores, spread like wildfire, and shut us down. I was devastated by the news, the stream of lives lost, the collective anguish. I was sleeping about four hours a night, wondering if this apocalyptic period would ever end, yet I was also deeply aware that now was the time to buy the dip. I had studied every crisis that led to a crash, and I knew that millionaires were born during these times. So I put my thinking cap on and began to apply everything I knew to this crash. I paid attention to the news and thought, *This is coming for us. This is it. This is the entrance I've been waiting for.* The chance to purchase the next few stocks I had had my eye on for the past couple of years was fast approaching. I pleaded for my closest friends and family to open brokerage accounts and take advantage of this opportunity, but they thought I was not thinking straight.

Meanwhile, I was smack in the middle of fulfilling my money intention with my Netflix stock. In late 2019, I decided to sell a third of my Netflix stock and use it as a down payment for our future home in Dallas. That amounted to about $100,000. But a few months later, when I read that the virus had hit Italy and was spreading fast, I pivoted my strategy and turned to Alfonso and said, "I know this isn't what we had originally planned, because this money is for a down payment for a house, but there's a big opportunity heading our way and you're going to have to trust me." The market hit bottom on March 23, 2020, and I was ready and waiting to redeploy my Netflix gains into new stocks.

What none of us saw coming was that in less than a month, we'd be privy to an aggressive bull market—a.k.a. a bull run—when the market soars and typically sees new all-time highs. My years of research, patience, and growing self-confidence in this space paid off big time. A lot of people made tons of money during this time. Then, months after the pandemic first hit, interest rates dropped, and that's when I sold another third of my Netflix stock, which had grown exponentially due to the bull run, to get back on track with buying our house, which we purchased in late 2020.

After close to eight years of owning Netflix stock, I managed to sell two big chunks of my shares and reinvest them in new stocks and a house while securing my initial investment, which means I have not lost a cent of the money I put into the stock, even though it took a downturn. I feel so proud of what I was able to accomplish with one stock. First step, invest. Next step, reinvest!

## GET READY TO SERVE A FEAST

As we move through our own growth and development within the market, it is important for us to process that our participation in this space will impact not only our own subconscious beliefs—a crucial component to our success—but also those of our closest friends and family members. I want you to know that I take teaching this material very seriously. When I called my closest family members to share what participating in the stock market could do for them, only my daughter and cousin took action. So I took my perspective to my Instagram stories and to community members on Patreon. The response was overwhelming. People wanted to know more; they wanted resources; they wanted to know where to start. Their enthusiasm brought me back to how hard it had been for me to enter this space, and I didn't want them to have to go through the same uphill struggle. So I poured everything I knew into a step-by-step course on how to open a brokerage account, never imagining it would turn into the movement and community resource it is today.

I believe that together we are changing a stagnant dynamic that has been in desperate need of our attention and action. I recently had a coaching call with some of my students, who are mostly people of color, and my jaw dropped to the ground when they shared their account pages. They went from never investing in the stock market before to having portfolios worth $100,000. Tears filled my eyes as I came to terms with their personal growth. There was real money in their lives now.

My philosophies and perspective will continue to evolve, and I will continue to learn and be a student. But one thing is clear: those who are able to tolerate the down days will be rewarded with the glory from the up days. So allow yourself to imagine more! Houses will be purchased, tuition will be paid, the next generation will learn about the stock market early on from us without the need of a step-by-step book to overcome their money wounds, and freedom will finally be obtained. We won't get rich overnight; we'll become wealthy over time.

# THE GREATEST TRANSFER
# OF WEALTH AND
# POWER STARTS NOW

We playing the long game. We don't want the money to
stop when we go.
When we can't work no more. We want it to outlive us,
we want it to be generational.

—*Nipsey Hussle*

A transfer of wealth usually happens in turbulent times. Money
leaves old hands and makes its way to new ones during every
geopolitical and global crisis, recession, and economic collapse
we experience. I learned this when we went through the 2008
housing crisis. I didn't have the means or know-how to invest
in the stock market yet, so I stood on the sidelines and watched

how many people navigated this emotional and financial roller coaster and managed to amass wealth. As the years rolled on, I realized that the transfer of wealth isn't a sprint; it's a steady long-distance warrior expedition across an expansive field. In stock market terms, an extended period of time when stocks are on the rise is called a bull run. Like any other expedition, there are those who participate, those who are still in training mode and not ready to jump in yet, those who see the warriors off from the safety of their home front, and those who have no clue an expedition is even taking place.

These turbulent times proved to be a catalyst for "the greatest transfer of wealth," a phrase that I began using as I witnessed money leaving old hands and reaching new ones. Suddenly, after ninety-two years on the list, ExxonMobil, once the largest company in the Dow, was removed from this index. A couple of weeks later, Etsy, the website where we get our cool shirts and handmade crafts, was ushered into the S&P 500. That was the transfer of wealth in the making before our eyes.

Furthermore, for the first time since I had started studying and participating in the market, I noticed a new and thrilling marker: more people of color were entering this space than ever before. I believe it has a lot to do with where we're at with technology and social media. The information needed to participate in the stock market has always been open to the public, but for years it had been living on sites like Bloomberg or Yahoo Finance, spaces that we didn't even know existed or couldn't access because they weren't geared toward us. But social media changed that. I remember when CNBC, a news station that broadcasts only stock market news during the day, used to move the market with its reporting, and now the power to push a stock up or down is being transferred to those on YouTube, Reddit, TikTok, and Twitter. According to a PwC report, Latines use their smartphones and apps more than any other demographic, and Pew Research Center reported that more Latines rely solely on their phones to access the internet than any other demographic. So when financial news began to pop up across our timelines, it became much more accessible to us than back in 1999 or even 2008.

Now we aren't just starting the greatest transfer of wealth; it's also an incredible transfer of power. As new shareholders, we have the power to vote on decisions made within the companies we've invested in. I dove into this opportunity head-on and not just as a marathon runner in the stock market. After I realized that urging my circle to invest wasn't convincing enough, I decided to create Wealth Rules Everything Around Me, my first course ever, to get more people in my community to face their money wounds and open a brokerage account—the catalyst to the creation of this book! I later found out that eight out of ten entrepreneurs who founded e-commerce businesses in 2020 were Latine, and a survey from Charles Schwab and Ariel Investments found that 30 percent of Black investors under thirty entered the stock market for the first time in 2020.

That's exactly why I believe this moment in time, as with other bear markets, recessions, or major geopolitical events, is a reset opportunity for us all. A chance to participate in a movement of wealth and power that has never been as accessible to us before. And I'm not talking access in terms of knowledge; I'm talking the start of a bull run where stocks are low and buying season is in session. Bull runs usually last around ten years and start right after the crisis hits. So don't get no FOMO, Warrior. It's 2023 and we're just making it to the starting line. Do your homework, set your rules, create your exit plan, and then get in the race when you're good and ready. Walk if you can't run. There's no shame in that. Just put one foot in front of the other and begin to participate. I don't want to do this alone. I want everyone and their mother to participate. There's plenty to go around. The greatest transfer of wealth is here; let's work together to make it permanent and long lasting.

## MODEL A SHIFT IN MINDSET: FROM GATEKEEPERS TO OPEN SOURCES

It was early 2020. I was sitting in our living room with my three-year-old son, Benicio, watching a kids' wrestling movie. The main characters were eating in a diner when a man walked in, stuck his hand under his coat to simulate a gun, and screamed at the cashier, "Give me all your money!" Some of the kids hid under the table, others looked on to figure out how to stop this man, and suddenly Benicio began to well up with emotion. He paused the movie and turned to me.

"Mom, I feel so bad for him."

"Who do you feel bad for?" I asked, wondering if he was referring to the person behind the counter getting robbed or one of the scared kids.

"The man that's robbing the diner," he replied.

"Why do you feel bad for him?"

"Because he's just looking for money, Mom. His only problem is that he doesn't know how to get money and he neeeeds it."

"Yeah, you're right," I said, slightly taken aback by his answer. "So how do you think he should get money?"

"The stock market," he said, as if that were the obvious response.

That's when I understood I had already started modeling a shift in mindset at home without even realizing it. My son was growing up in this energy and space, seeing money from a completely different perspective than my own, my mom's, and my grandmother's. He wasn't in scarcity mode, he didn't fear money, and he was already seeing money as a tool rather than an emotionally charged superior controlling our lives. That's long-lasting generational wealth right there, something he will later be able to pass on to his kids, grandkids, friends, community. That's what I want for all of us now. Remember: wealth doesn't just come in the form of money; it's also knowledge. And knowledge is power.

A couple of years earlier, I had finally decided to come out as an investor to my podcast listeners, friends, and family. Fear had pushed me to hide this journey from everyone except Bricia, Patty, and Alfonso. I didn't want to be scared out of the market, and I didn't want to be judged. So I had secret conversations with my money-conscious fam about my participation. Guilt followed me around like a lost puppy, shaming me for not sharing this big secret about financial freedom I was uncovering, but fear of judgment kept me quiet. I also thought that part of opening up about my stock market journey would imply telling people what to invest in, and I didn't want to take on that responsibility. I was also afraid of being seen as less honorable because I was making easy money instead of working hard for it, yet not sharing this valuable information made me feel low-key greedy. False beliefs and money wounds abounded.

But with time and experience, I realized that not talking about it openly was turning me into a defensive gatekeeper of the market. And that made me no better than the system at large, which has kept us out of investing through fearmongering and silencing. So I decided to flip the script and become an open source for my community so that they too could press the reset button on their financial path and join this space. And the response was absolutely exhilarating. So many people reached out expressing curiosity about the stock market and wanting to know more. Funnily enough, I was so focused on the relief of finally coming out publicly as an investor that it took me two years and the start of a pandemic to work through my new crop of money wounds and realize there was a business opportunity here, a hunger that needed to be fed, and a chance for me to pass the torch and distribute this light to many more members of my community and beyond. Now I hope that you will join me in spreading the word, leading by example, and sharing your feast.

Start by sharing your journey with your circle. Have open conversations, and show them the intentions you set, what you've accomplished so far within your time horizon, and what your goals are in the long term. You may be met with resistance at first, because change or anything new is scary to all of us, but don't retreat. The best way to show the positive effects that investing has on your confidence and your pocket is to model the behavior, share your resources and knowledge, and aim to normalize this conversation. Give them a peek at your portfolio over a specific time frame, the way my colleague did with me at Netflix. There's nothing like seeing the numbers with your own eyes. Let it sink in, answer any questions, make it a safe space for them, direct people to the appropriate resources, and maybe add something like "This is possible for you too. The stock market is not unique to me."

I know the high of exploring and sharing the stock market is tremendous, but the last thing I want you to do is force or shame anyone into entering the market, because that will defy our collective purpose—to bring more people from communities of color into this all-important fold with love and respect. Remember: each person's path is different. Our needs are different. Our comfort levels are different. And our money wounds are different. So we must respect these differences and create a safe space where others feel welcome and comfortable. Eventually, you'll notice that some people will naturally gravitate toward you and ask things like "Hey, I have this money. What should I do with it?" That's your opening to share resources and model your behavior in this space. Talk with them about those wealth-generating investments we explored in Step 2, share what inspired you to enter the market, make yourself vulnerable, and tell them about your mistakes and how you chose to handle the cramps or thirst you may have felt midway through the expedition. Normalize those peaks and valleys to help them shed some of their own fears and misconceptions about the market. This will be your way of showing them the expedition taking place and modeling behavior that can potentially drive change and expansion in our communities of color. Then it will be up to them to choose if they prefer to be a spectator, a trainee, or a participant.

## SHARE AND EXPAND YOUR BOUNTIFUL FEAST

By sharing your knowledge and resources, you've already started sharing your feast. Keep doing what you're doing, and when you're ready, take it up a notch. I began by sharing my journey with my money-conscious fam, then I opened up to my community about it. I'm building generational wealth for my daughter and son, and now I'm ideating other ways to share my feast. For example, one of my next goals is to use a portion of my gains to purchase an investment property and turn it into a short-term rental venture. When my aunt and uncle, my cousin Juanita's parents, heard me talk about this, they immediately jumped in with a supportive "Tú puedes, mija. Yo te ayudo a manejar el ter- reno. You can do it! I'll work for you—let's make it happen!" They had witnessed my journey up close. My uncle was one of the ones who called me out on being addicted to shopping in my early twenties and pushed me to open my eyes on that front. Then my aunt, uncle, and Juanita noticed I paid attention to them, and they watched my dedication to self-improvement develop and push me past the wounds I had been carrying for so long and into new and bountiful territory. They have always believed in me. Suddenly, buying this piece of land and developing this new project meant that I could finally pay it forward by sharing and expanding this feast with them. The battlefield is at long last turning into a bountiful financial garden that I can share with others beyond my immediate family—generational and communal wealth-building in full force.

Now my favorite sport is watching my community build wealth. I have students who've used their gains for a down payment on a home or to invest in a business. One couple bought a gym and the necessary equipment to have it fully functioning. Each of these ventures feeds into bettering our lives and our communities as a whole. This means we have the chance to reap the rewards of our discipline, knowledge, and dedication and feast with our family and beyond. This needs to be one of the main goals in the center of the intentions driving us forward. Not because money is everything. Because freedom is everything. Because options are everything. The combination of money, freedom, and options opens up time and space in our lives to focus on creating long-lasting change.

At the end of the day, it's not about the feast itself. It's about all the moments that lead up to your feast. The time you spend monitoring your thoughts and actions and calling out your scarcity mindset. The process of witnessing yourself emotionally detach from money. The day you realize money is a tool and you decide to put that tool to work for you. The sense of achievement you feel after holding your own in a conversation about the stock market with your colleagues in the break room. That change, growth, and evolution that happens with each and every one of these moments in your journey is so much more empowering than the money itself. It's the journey that bolsters your self-esteem and allows you to break generational money traumas so that the only hand-me-downs your descendants will receive are wealth-generating assets and wealth-building inspiration.

I don't want to reach this peak on my own; I set out to show you my process, my story, my gains, and my losses to encourage you to be the person I wish I could've seen in my community. I want to see more people of color become millionaires, more Latinas generating bountiful wealth. I want to see a time when we have more access to venture capital so that we too are funded. So that we too can create publicly traded companies and have our own people investing in and utilizing our businesses. The stock market is no longer a secret society; it's an open-source community where everyone is welcome. I want us to turn each expedition into a relay race where we continuously pass the baton to future generations. We have a lot of work to do together. This is a call to action, my Wealth Warriors. And it's only the beginning!

# ACKNOWLEDGMENTS

Opening up about investing in the stock market and what I've learned along the way has been by far the scariest task I've ever felt called to execute. What this process has taught me is that the experience I am having now is possible only because there was an army of warriors that have shaped, guided, and protected this experience.

To my agent, Johanna Castillo, thank you for believing in this journey and making sure it is shared as far as we could collectively reach. I am not sure what I did in life to have such a powerful being like you representing me, but I receive it with an open heart.

To my publisher, Krishan Trotman, thank you for continuously stepping into your personal power and amplifying the voices of our communities. You gave me permission to show up exactly as I am, in a space where I perceived that my I AM would not be welcomed.

To my editor, Amina Iro, thank you for all your hard work on a topic that is so layered and complex. You pushed me to stretch and elevate the book to new heights with our communities always top of mind.

To all the Legacy Lit fam, thank you for your contribution and hard work in making the book happen.

To Cecilia Molinari, mi hermana de la luna, you had me at doodle. Thank you for jumping into my world with both feet as you took on the challenge to start your own Wealth Warrior journey. We were comrades exploring the battlefield and searching for all the ways that we could best describe the blueprint.

To Claudia Munoz and Mari Brambila, you saw the vision and moved toward it with no questions asked. I could not operate this without you. Thank you for the inspiration to continue when I wanted to give up and for protecting my space when I needed to dive deeper into this manuscript.

A mi ángel Gavino Figueroa, yo sé que usted vio mi camino antes de que yo lo viera. Gracias por siempre estar conmigo protegiéndome.

To my daughter, Elizabeth Ruiz, you were the catalyst for change in my life. You are my shero. I would not be where I am today without you.

To my son, Benicio Ayala, you have stayed true to your name and have brought with you so many blessings into all our lives. Your presence alone has removed so many experiences of limitations.

To my partner, Alfonso Ayala, thank you for always pushing me into my higher self, for respecting my higher self, and for loving my higher self. And thank you for consistently holding our family down and for keeping me grounded when I face my panic and anxiety.

To my Sissy Darlene García, thank you for always centering family in the way that you do. My favorite part of our journey has been the one where we both are mothers alongside one another. Hector Lemus, thank you for being the supportive big brother

I never had. To my Emi and Jordy Lemus, I will forever honor my title as tía Sissy, please know that always and forever you can count on me to cheer you on and be here for all the love and support.

Madre, you are the original Wealth Warrior, thank you for teaching me how to work hard and commit to what I want to achieve. Thank you for always doing your absolute best with what you could. I honor every single part of your journey.

To my cousin Juanita Morfin, the problem solver, the caretaker, la más chingona. I know it has not always been easy to take on this responsibility for all of us. I honor you. This journey wouldn't even exist if it wasn't for your diligence in wanting me to get my shit together financially.

Tía Tonia, tía Lupe, tío Mariano, tía Ramon, no saben ustedes cuánto los quiero. Siempre me han tratado como a una hija y desde niña chiquita que siento su amor.

To Melissa, we did it. We got to so many of the places we always dreamed we would. My OG partner in life, you are my sister in journey; some of the most fun experiences in life were alongside you. Little Cami, you came here to kick butt; I am so proud of your accomplishments at such a young age!

To my aunt Irene and uncle Enrique, thank you for the demonstration of an entrepreneurial spirit and the representation of luxury.

To Juanito Diaz, I see so much of myself in your lived experiences. Thank you for always having my back. I will always have yours. I can't wait for the world to meet you.

To my compadre José Rodríguez, te quiero un chingo, gracias

por todo tu amor incondicional y por la manifestación de tu ahijado.

Daniel Pacheco, if it wasn't for you, I would have never learned to appreciate the art of film. I would have never journeyed to Lionsgate and on to Netflix; thank you.

To Jerry Martinez, nunca se me van a olvidar las pláticas que tuvimos en un entonces cuando todo se sentía oscuro. Tú siempre fuiste luz. Gracias por estar presente para Elizabeth en tiempos que no pude estar.

To Mr. and Mrs. Ekstrom, Gigi and Johan, there's so much I want the world to know about the two of you. The fact that people like you even exist tells me all I need to know about how extraordinary Source is. Thank you for taking me into the New York Stock Exchange when I was seventeen years old. Thank you for taking me into your home. Thank you for the incredible meals on the deck. Thank you for teaching me to savor life in between each bite and each sip. Thank you for teaching me what family can look like. Thank you for establishing rules and discipline. I feel incredibly grateful that I got to experience that above all else. It's true what they say about children just wanting structure. Having to read one book a week is what got me here today. Writing your names in the acknowledgments of this book feels like something that lives in between destiny and the divine. My greatest accomplishment will be *Wealth Warrior* taking up space in your library of books. I cannot say thank you enough. You have deeply impacted me and so many others. I love you always and forever, your First Daughter, Linda.

To Minus Won, Brenda Rios, you live on in my heart.

To Andy García, my CPA, my brother from another mother. You truly make a dream team, the real MVP. Thank you for so openly taking the time to educate all of us on money.

To Nick Levin, thank you for taking the time to educate me on stocks and not gate keep; you have taught me to do the same.

To Nadine Dennis, my girl, you always kept it one hundred with me. Thank you for teaching me how to unapologetically use money and not let it use me.

To Patty Rodriguez, one of my greatest joys is to mastermind with you and bend the universe in ways we did not know were possible. I love our visits to the moon together. Don't ever forget that half of the moon is yours and the other half is mine.

To Bricia Lopez, thank you for always teaching me to own my desires and let go of any shame when it comes to money.

To Ana Flores, Cosmic Christine, and Dari Luna, the three of you have created important portals for me in this journey. You set the stage and pushed me to walk through.

To Maricela Camarena Aleti and Yesenia Armijo Mendez, twenty-seven years ago you all began teaching me to be a much better version of myself. Both of you have been there during crucial moments in my life, like two pillars, stable, grounded, and intricate, demonstrating how strong I too can be. From cheer and drill camp to being leaders in high school and going off to explore the trails of Europe, you were the first peers who showed me the possibilities outside of our hood. You taught me to reach with confidence and aggressively. To not cower. Maricela, I always wanted to be like you. You always were there guiding me in all areas of my life. Everything I reached for, like working at TDW, being on the drill team, joining DECA, and becoming senior class vice president, was because of you. Thank you for bringing Gigi into my life.

And last but certainly not least, thank you to our In Luz We Trust money-conscious fam, the army of Wealth Warriors. To those who have been there from the start and to those who are joining us now, this book would not be possible if it wasn't for each and every one of you pushing for more resources and always reminding me how much we need more material like this. Thank you for always believing in me and opening the space for all of us.

xo

Linda

# WEALTH WARRIOR
## STOCK MARKET GLOSSARY

**after-market hours:** After-market hours are Monday to Friday from 4:00 p.m. to 8:00 p.m. ET.

**annual percentage yield (APY):** The rate of return earned on an investment, taking into account the compound interest.

**appreciates:** Increases in value or price.

**asset:** Something that puts money into your wallet, such as stocks, bonds, income-generating real estate, and a business that does not require your presence.

**balance sheet:** A financial statement that reports a company's assets, liabilities, and shareholders' equity.

**bear/bearish:** A general sentiment or feeling that the stock market is downtrending and will continue to downtrend.

**bear market:** A sustained 20 percent decline in the stock market for two months or more specifically tracked on the S&P 500 index.

**beneficiary:** A person or entity who will receive your high-yield savings accounts, IRAs, HSAs, and brokerage accounts once you pass away.

**blue chip stocks:** Stocks of well-known, high-quality companies that are leaders in their industry and have stood the test of time.

**bottom line:** The net income that is free and clear of costs and expenses.

**brokerage account:** An investment account that gives you access to the stock market and allows you to purchase stocks, bonds, IRAs, and other types of securities.

**brokerage firm:** A company that brings buyers and sellers together to expedite their transactions in the stock market.

**bull/bullish:** A general sentiment or feeling that the stock market is uptrending and will continue to uptrend.

**bull market:** When the S&P 500 index is up by 20 percent from the most recent low, with no sign of a downturn.

**capital gains:** The profit earned on the sale of an asset that has increased in value over the holding period.

**cash flow statement:** A financial statement that reflects changes in a balance sheet pertaining to cash and cash equivalents.

**catalyst:** An event that leads to a substantial change in a stock's current price, positive or negative.

**CDP score:** The CDP (formerly the Carbon Disclosure Project) assesses and discloses a company's environmental impact.

**certified public accountant (CPA):** A member of an officially accredited professional body of accountants.

**compound interest:** The amount you earn on both the principal and the interest accrued.

**cost basis:** The average value of all the shares you own.

**cost of goods sold (COGS):** This tells us the cost of producing the goods or services sold by a company.

**current ratio:** An equation calculated by dividing a company's current assets by its current liabilities. The current ratio lets us know the health of the business and how long it could sustain itself if the business had to shut down.

**cyclical stocks:** Stocks that have seasons and may also be more immediately affected by the health of the economy. Examples are airlines, retail, hotels, and restaurants.

**defensive stocks:** Stocks that pertain to well-established companies, like those in the blue chip category, that provide consistent dividends and stable earnings regardless of the state of the overall stock market.

**depreciation:** The decrease in monetary value of an asset due to use, wear and tear, or obsolescence.

**dividend:** A distribution (payment) made from a company's earnings to its shareholders.

**dividend stocks:** Stocks that reward you with a dividend when they generate profits.

**dividend yield:** The dividend yield is a ratio that is composed of the current stock price and the total dividend amount over the last year.

**Dow Jones Industrial Average:** An index that is used to track the price of each share of thirty publicly traded blue chip companies.

**earnings call:** A conference call where executives from a publicly traded company discuss their quarterly financial statements as well as provide guidance for the company's future.

**earnings seasons:** The four quarters of each year when financial statements are made public.

**employee stock options:** The option to own shares from your place of employment.

**EPS (earnings per share):** This figure is calculated by dividing the net income of a company by its outstanding shares—that is, the amount of shares the company has issued for distribution/ownership—and it shows how profitable a company is per share.

**equity:** In accounting, it represents assets minus liabilities. Equity in homeownership is your loan amount minus the worth of the house. Equity in stocks is the price purchased minus the current value of the stock. Equity in a startup is a percentage of ownership in the company and future growth.

**estate planning:** The process of planning the management and distribution of a person's assets after death.

**ETF:** An exchange-traded fund, a basket of stocks that trades similarly to individual stocks but is not limited to one industry.

**FDIC:** The Federal Deposit Insurance Corporation, or the FDIC, is an independent federal agency that safeguards your deposits in the event that your bank fails because of economic downturn. The standard maximum insurable amount for an FDIC-insured account is $250,000.

**fifty-two-week high:** This indicates the highest price point the share has reached and closed at within the last fifty-two weeks.

**fifty-two-week low:** This indicates the lowest the share price has reached and closed at in the last fifty-two weeks.

**financial portfolio:** A grouping of financial assets such as stocks, bonds, currencies, et cetera.

**FOMO:** An acronym for fear of missing out, used when a stock is experiencing a massive share price increase.

**fractional shares:** Shares that are pieces or fractions of a full share of a company or ETF.

**fundamental analysis:** The use of revenues, earnings, future growth, return on equity, and profit margins, as well as other data to determine the value of a company and its potential for future growth.

**gross profit:** This is the revenue minus cost of goods sold (COGs).

**growth stocks:** Stocks that offer substantially higher growth above the overall market average.

**health savings account (HSA):** A type of savings account for use with qualified healthcare expenses.

**high-yield savings account:** A savings account that typically pays twenty to twenty-five times more than a regular savings account.

**income statement:** Also known as a profit and loss statement, this shows us the company's revenue, cost of goods sold, and expenses, including any operational costs to run the business over a period of time, and lets us know how the company is performing in generating revenue and how efficient it is with operating expenses.

**index:** A grouping of stocks that meet specific criteria to serve as a benchmark to track the movement of the market, allowing us to compare current price levels to past ones so that we can see the market's overall performance and measure the health of the economy.

**inflation:** The decrease in the purchasing power of money, which is measured by how much more expensive a set of goods and services has become over a period of time.

**interest:** The price paid to borrow money.

**large cap stocks:** Companies with a market capitalization of $10 billion or more—they're considered safer and more conservative investments.

**liability:** Something that takes money out of your wallet, such as mortgages, car loans, credit cards, debt, and taxes.

**long-term horizon:** An investment goal or strategy to hold an asset for more than ten years and as long as twenty or more years.

**long-term investment:** An investment that you plan to keep for at least a year.

**market capitalization:** The value of a publicly traded company determined by multiplying the total number of shares the company offers by the current share price.

**market correction:** A market decline that is more than 10 percent but less than 20 percent on the S&P 500 index.

**market crash:** When the market drops drastically from a major catastrophic event or the collapse of a speculative bubble.

**market hours:** Traditional market hours are Monday to Friday from 9:30 a.m. to 4:00 p.m. ET.

**market sectors:** There are eleven different trading categories in the market, known as sectors, where you can find similar goods and services: information technology, healthcare, financials, consumer discretionary, communication services, industrials, consumer staples, energy, utilities, real estate, and materials.

**market tuition:** When losses on an investment are a realized loss (see *realized gains and losses*) and you have lost money in the stock market. The lessons learned from the loss are considered tuition paid to the stock market.

**meme stocks:** Stocks that have gone viral with massive overnight growth. In many cases, these are organized efforts by trading communities like Wall Street Bets.

**mid cap stocks:** Companies with a market capitalization between $2 billion and $10 billion. These are considered riskier than large cap stocks but have more room for future growth.

**Nasdaq Composite index:** An index that tracks primarily technology stocks, like the famous FANG (Facebook, Amazon, Netflix, and Google).

**net income:** Operating income minus interest and taxes, in other words, money that is free and clear of costs and expenses.

**operating profit** (EBIT, earnings before interest and taxes): This is gross profit minus operating expenses.

**penny stocks:** Stocks that trade for less than five dollars per share.

**pre-market hours:** Pre-market hours are Monday to Friday from 4:00 a.m. to 9:30 a.m. ET.

**price-to-earnings (P/E) ratio:** This number indicates how much investors pay per dollar of a company's earnings annually. For example, if a company's P/E ratio is 15, that means the shares cost 15 times the profit the company makes on a per-share basis a year.

**principal:** The amount of money borrowed.

**publicly traded company:** Also known as a public company, publicly held company, publicly listed company, or public limited company, this is a company whose ownership is held via those who own shares of their stock.

**pump and dump:** When a group of experienced traders organizes in chat communities like Reddit and Discord to purposely pump up a stock, creating buzz around it in the news, so that a ton of typically inexperienced investors will buy in quickly and drive the stock up to new all-time highs. That's when the experienced traders take immediate action and sell out—dump the stock—multiplying their money, while the mix of inexperienced investors who did not do their research are left on the losing side.

**realized gains and losses:** The amount of money either lost or gained from the sale of a share.

**retail investor:** An individual investor who buys and sells stock.

**retained earnings:** The amount of profit a company has left over after paying out all costs and income taxes, as well as its dividends to shareholders.

**reticular activating system (RAS):** A collection of neurons located in the brain stem that receives input on everything that activates our senses.

**revenue:** Money generated from goods and services sold.

**reverse stock split:** A reduction in the number of a company's traded shares that results in an increase in the per value or earnings per share.

**Roth IRA:** An individual retirement account funded by after-tax dollars.

**Securities and Exchange Commission (SEC):** An independent agency of the US government that regulates the stock market and protects investors.

**shareholders' equity:** A company's assets minus its liabilities, which represents the company's net worth.

**shares:** Representations of the fractional ownership of a publicly traded company.

**short-term horizon:** An investment goal or strategy to hold an asset for less than ten years.

**short-term investment:** An investment that you keep for less than a year.

**simple interest:** The amount earned on the initial principal borrowed or deposited. Simple interest accounts typically pertain to a mortgage, car loan, or bank account, depending on the bank.

**small cap stocks:** Companies with a market capitalization below $2 billion. These are considered riskier than mid caps but have even more room for future growth.

**speculative stocks:** Stocks that are extremely high risk; the investment outcome is mere speculation, as the fundamentals of the company do not reflect its potential strength.

**Standard and Poor's 500 (S&P 500):** The Standard and Poor's 500 index tracks the top 500 companies listed on the Nasdaq exchange or the New York Stock Exchange. It is the index most commonly used to reflect the US stock market and the economy overall.

**stock:** The shares of a publicly traded company.

**stock chart:** A graph that shows information, such as the price and purchase volume, on how a publicly traded company is performing over different periods of time.

**stock exchange:** The infrastructure that facilitates the trading of equity securities or stocks. This provides a formal mechanism where shares are listed and exchange transactions are made. Stock exchanges can be electronic or manual and they provide pertinent information about the size of the stock market.

**stock market:** Where investors or traders connect to buy and sell shares of ownership in a publicly traded company. Well-known exchanges in the stock market are the New York Stock Exchange and the Nasdaq.

**stock market bubble:** A type of economic bubble taking place in stock markets when market participants drive stock prices above their value.

**stock market investor:** A person who purchases shares and holds them for the long term with the expectation of generating profit.

**stock market trader:** A person who purchases shares and holds the shares for the short term (minutes, days, weeks, or months) with the expectation of generating a profit.

**stock split:** The decision of a company to increase the number of shares by issuing more shares.

**stonks:** An intentional misspelling of the word *stocks*. The term is used in a humorous way, underlining the losses incurred typically by meme stocks and making fun of the lack of knowledge shown by newer investors.

**technical analysis:** The use of historical market data, including price and volume, with the use of charts to predict the future movements of the price for potential profit.

**tech stocks:** Any stock involved in the technology sector, from semiconductor producers to software providers.

**ticker symbol:** Also known as a stock symbol, this is a unique series of letters assigned to a publicly traded company and is used to identify the stock at the time of purchase.

**time horizon:** The period of time one expects to hold an investment. Time horizons are determined by investment goals and strategies.

**top line:** The amount of revenue that has come into the company.

**traditional IRA:** An individual retirement account funded by pre-tax dollars.

**unrealized gains and losses:** Also known as "paper" gains/losses, this is the dollar amount that you are either up or down on the shares you've purchased but not yet sold.

**value stocks:** Stocks that have grown into industry leaders, with little room for future growth but seen by many as reliable business models that are undervalued.

**volatility:** Volatility is when a stock rises and falls sharply with big swings on the upside and big swings on the downside.

# RESOURCES

Following is a list of resources to further enhance your Wealth Warrior journey beyond these pages.

## Join me in a deeper dive into the stock market:

STACKS: https://inluzwetrust.teachable.com/p/stacks
WREAM: https://inluzwetrust.teachable.com/p/wream
Money Masterwork: https://inluzwetrust.teachable.com/p
 /masterwork
The Power of the Stock Market: inluzwetrust.teachable.com/p
 /the-power-of-the-stock-market

## Useful sites:

Investopedia for terms: https://www.investopedia.com/
Yahoo Finance for charts and news: https://finance.yahoo.com/
Finviz for heatmap, which takes the temperature of stocks in
 real time on the S&P 500: https://finviz.com/
CNBC for stock market news: https://www.cnbc.com/
Earnings Whispers for earnings updates: https://www
 .earningswhispers.com/
Seeking Alpha for stock news: https://seekingalpha.com/

## Community groups:

ILWT Newsletter: https://www.inluzwetrust.com/contact

Patreon with Discord access: https://www.patreon.com
/inluzwetrust

ILWT Instagram: https://www.instagram.com/inluzwetrust/

Luz Warrior Instagram: https://www.instagram.com/luzwarrior/

ILWT Twitter: https://twitter.com/inluzwetrust

Investies Podcast: https://www.inluzwetrust.com//investiespodcast

Let There Be Luz Podcast: https://podcasts.apple.com/us
/podcast/let-there-be-luz/id1278718509

## Five books I recommend you check out:

*My Stock Market Workbook* by Elizabeth Ruiz and Linda Garcia

*The Abundance Book* by John Randolph Price

*The Richest Man in Babylon* by George S. Clason

*The Law of Divine Compensation: On Work, Money, and
Miracles* by Marianne Williamson

*Think and Grow Rich* by Napoleon Hill

For more options, check out my entire list at: https://www
.amazon.com/shop/luzwarrior/list/5QHZY2DBAC9K?ref_=aip
_sf_list_spv_ofs_mixed_d